Journey to the cross

D0762581

Journey
to the cross

God's amazing plan of salvation

Roger Ellsworth

 **EVANGELICAL PRESS**

EVANGELICAL PRESS
Grange Close, Faverdale North Industrial Estate, Darlington,
Co. Durham, DL3 0PH, England

First published 1997

British Library Cataloguing in Publication Data available

ISBN 0 85234 397 3

Printed and bound in Great Britain by Creative Print and Design
Wales, Ebbw Vale.

The following chapters are affectionately dedicated to the memory of the two people who first taught me to love the cross of Christ,
my parents, William C. and Erma Ellsworth.

Contents

Section II: On the cross

Section III: From the cross

Section IV: Responding to the journey

Preface

I was a mere child when I came to love the cross of Christ. I attribute that love to nothing less than the sheer grace of God that worked in my young heart.

God does, of course, have his instruments. In my case, he used my dear parents and faithful pastors to instil that love in my heart. I will be for ever grateful for these lovers of the cross.

In those early years I never imagined that I would venture to write a book on the cross, but venture I must. As I send out these chapters, I am keenly aware that there are many others who have done much to make them possible. I am grateful for all these. I have been immensely helped by other authors who have travelled this ground before me. I consider these chapters to be my faint 'Amen!' to these giants of the cross.

I must also express gratitude to the dear souls who make up my beloved Immanuel family. These folk have frequently and gladly journeyed to the cross with me over the years.

I am also grateful for the editors of Evangelical Press who have been very patient, kind and helpful in making this work possible, all of which I appreciate very much. As always, I am indebted to my wife, Sylvia, and to my secretary, Sheila Ketteman, for their encouragement and assistance. I especially appreciate the assistance of Diana Zinzilieta in preparing these chapters.

I hope and pray that what follows will be of such a nature that those of us who have cast ourselves on Christ's atoning death will find our love flaming higher and burning brighter as we again follow our Lord there and marvel at the sight of redeeming love that paid for us so high a price.

Roger Ellsworth
Benton, Illinois,
August 1997

Introduction

My purpose in these chapters is to trace the steps of the most astonishing journey in all the annals of history. That journey began in the counsels of the triune God in eternity past. It is the journey of Jesus Christ to the cross where he was crucified. It is not enough, however, only to journey as far as the cross. We must also contemplate what took place there and what it produced. Our journey is, therefore, to the cross and beyond.

That cross is the focal point of human history. When it was raised against the sky, it split history in half. All that took place before the moment when Jesus died there must be seen in terms of his relentless approach to keep that appointment made in eternity past. All that occurred subsequent to his appointment with the cross must be viewed in the light of what he accomplished there.

Martyn Lloyd-Jones says of the cross of Christ, 'It was the most momentous hour since the beginning of the world, it is indeed the turning-point which determines everything — it is the greatest event, the most ... climactic event that has ever taken place in this world. Everything leads up to that hour, everything eventuates from that hour. That is the hour to which the whole of prophecy is looking forward, and to which the whole of the church, and her doctrine and history look back. It is the central, focal, point which determines and controls everything.'[1]

Why is it important to trace Jesus' steps to and from the cross? Why is it important to know that the cross was planned in eternity past, that Jesus steadily approached it throughout his public ministry and now, along with his Father and his people, looks back upon it with complete satisfaction?

A sense of awe and wonder

The first answer to that question must surely be to fill us with a sense of awe and wonder over the stunning greatness of our salvation and over the love of God that produced it.

One cannot read much of the New Testament without being impressed with how its authors exulted in the greatness of salvation through that cross. To them it was the most remarkable and glorious thing imaginable.

We find the apostle Paul writing, 'But God forbid that I should glory except in the cross of our Lord Jesus Christ, by whom the world has been crucified to me, and I to the world' (Gal. 6:14). In his first letter to the Corinthians, the apostle says, 'I determined not to know anything among you except Jesus Christ and him crucified' (1 Cor. 2:2). The author of Hebrews also gloried in the salvation provided by the cross of Christ by referring to it as 'so great a salvation' (Heb. 2:3).

On and on we could go with instances of the New Testament writers glorying in the cross of Christ. But it does not stop there. Those who followed the first-century Christians have gloried in it as well. In John Bunyan's *Pilgrim's Progress*, Christian carried a heavy load of guilt and sin until he came to the cross of Christ. There his burden fell off and rolled away. After that we read, 'Then he stood still awhile to look and wonder, for it was very surprising to him, that the sight of the cross should thus ease him of his burden. He looked therefore, and looked again, even till the springs that were in his head sent the waters down his cheeks...'[2]

The sceptics have always been astonished that anyone would dare suggest that eternal salvation is provided by a Jewish rabbi dying on a Roman cross. The Christian is astonished as well. He is astonished that it is all true. He says with Bunyan's Christian:

Thus far did I come laden with my sin,
Nor could aught ease the grief that I was in,
Till I came hither. What a place is this!
Must here be the beginning of my bliss!
Must here the burden fall from off my back!
Must here the strings that bound it to me crack!
Blest cross! blest sepulchre! blest rather be
The man that there was put to shame for me![3]

Yes, what a place is this!

As wondrous as the cross is, there are, amazingly enough, many indications that a sense of awe is missing from much of the church today. Our worship is often muffled and muted and characterized by a desire for the novel and entertaining. Startling, gigantic truths are sung with subdued tones. Sermons that handle those same truths often lead to suppressed — and sometimes unsuppressed — yawns. The same people who gasp in awe at an unusual feat in sports seem unable to summon even a little interest in the things of God. If we are honest, most of us would have to talk a long time before we ever got around to using the word 'awe' to describe how we feel about the things of God.

What is wrong with us? The plain truth is that most of us have never understood in anywhere near an adequate measure the vast scope of the plan of redemption. Much of the missing awe and wonder will return to the redeemed when they are made to see that they are caught up in something that stretches from eternity to eternity.

A return to priorities

Why is it important to trace Jesus' steps to and from the cross? A second answer is that this will call us back from the shallows and fringes to proclaim the central truths of the faith.

There are many indications that much of the professing church is indeed floundering in the shallows.

In his *God in the Wasteland*, David Wells deplores the current 'weightlessness' of God in the church. He writes, 'God rests too inconsequentially upon the church. His truth is too distant, his grace is too ordinary, his judgment is too benign, his gospel is too easy, and his Christ is too common.'[4] We could just as well speak of the 'weightlessness' of the cross.

Modern-day Christians are absorbed with themselves and their problems, and pastors, ever eager to keep the pews and the offering plates replenished, are content to give them what they want. Any pastor who dares to devote his pulpit ministry to those central doctrines that surround the cross will be apt to hear this rejoinder: 'I am not interested in all that stuff. Just tell me how to get through Monday.'

So, in the interest of getting their hearers through Monday, many pastors devote themselves entirely to 'life-management' preaching. Those great Old Testament stories that former generations understood as pointing to the cross of Christ are now suddenly found to yield profound psychological insights for coping with life and its various stresses and strains. Isaac and Rebekah (and David centuries later) are transformed into baby-boomers who struggle with child-rearing. Jacob becomes the hard-driving businessman who loses his sense of priorities. And Daniel and his friends become role models for dealing with peer pressure. While there are, of course, applications to be made along these lines, the tragedy of the pulpit in our day is that they are made without any reference at all to Christ and his cross. It is virtually forgotten these days that the cross of Christ is the grand theme of Scripture. Given the current climate, one wonders if we shall soon hear a sermon on animal rights, or how to handle pets, drawn from the account of Balaam and his donkey!

In his book, *Christ's Incredible Cross*, David Kirkwood laments the trend away from cross-centred preaching to crisis-centred preaching. In particular, he notes the emphasis on marriage seminars. He writes, 'I thank God for the marriages that have been helped and healed by this means, but can you imagine the Apostle Paul (or any of the apostles) visiting a local church to host a four-day marriage seminar? Can you imagine the listing of his sermon topics, such as "How to Understand Your Mate," and "How to Handle Disputes About Finances," and "How to Meet the Psychological Needs of Your Wife"?'[5]

When preachers do get around to dealing with the cross, the same psychological approach used in other Scriptures often comes into play. This makes the cross little more than a proof that we are important to God and should, therefore, face our problems with a marvellous sense of self-confidence and self-worth.

Churches and pastors often give the impression that the best way to handle the cross is through dramatic re-enactments of it — many of which are very lavish and elaborate. But after the drama is over, those who witnessed it have no more idea of what that crucifixion was all about than they had when they came. Only a clear understanding of the cross will produce that profound appreciation that will purge our lives of unworthy and meaningless priorities.

A sense of assurance

Tracing our Lord's journey to the cross will have the additional benefit of filling us with assurance. We shall come to understand that our salvation was mapped out in eternity past and that God has meticulously fulfilled that plan. We shall not then be able to doubt for a single moment that he will eventually bring us safely into his eternal glory.

Many today lack this assurance. They go hesitantly to heaven, wondering each step of the way if they will finally gain entrance there. Often their lack of assurance is because they wonder if their experience will measure up to what is required. Did they feel enough emotion when they made their profession of faith? What a relief it is to learn that our salvation rests, not on our having a perfect experience, but rather on Christ's experience on the cross! Doubts flee when we learn to fend off Satan's assaults by pointing him firmly to the cross of Christ.

These, and many other benefits as well, flow from a better understanding of the cross of Christ. My purpose in these chapters is to attempt to make the cross weigh more heavily upon us so that we can reap these benefits in fuller measure.

Section I
Towards the cross

When did the Son of God begin moving towards the cross on which he was finally crucified? When did he know that shameful death would be his?

Was it there in Gethsemane's dark garden when his sweat became as great drops of blood? Yes, and before that.

Was it when he rode into Jerusalem amidst the triumphant hosannas of the swelling multitude? Yes, and before that.

Was it there on Mt Tabor when he glistened with heaven's glory and spoke of his coming death with Moses and Elijah? Yes, and before that.

Was it when he heard John the Baptist decisively declare him to be the Lamb of God? Yes, and before that.

The testimony of Scripture is clear. The Son of God began his steady approach to the cross before the world began. That approach continued through the long centuries of the Old Testament and was pictured and prophesied during that time. In the fulness of time, the Son of God stepped onto the stage of human history as a mere baby for the express purpose of dying on that cross which he had been approaching from eternity past. He began his public ministry with that cross fully in view and unwaveringly approached it until, from its fiery anguish, he was able to cry triumphantly, 'It is finished!'

So the cross was no afterthought with God. It was not a matter of God resorting to Plan B after Plan A had failed. The cross was always Plan A, and there has never been a Plan B. God does not need a Plan B because his plans do not fail. To suggest that the cross was a last-minute stratagem that God was forced to accept by previously unforeseen circumstances is to say that God is not sovereign and is, therefore, not God.

The following chapters place the cross in eternity past and trace the Son's relentless approach to it.

Chapter 19 — The Son affirms the cross: Gethsemane
1. John Flavel, *The Works of John Flavel,* The Banner of Truth Trust, vol. i, p.275.
2. William Hendriksen, *New Testament Commentary: Matthew,* Baker Book House, p.918.
3. John Gill, *Exposition of Old & New Testaments,* The Baptist Standard Bearer, vol vii, p.335.
4. S. G. DeGraaf, *Promise and Deliverance,* Presbyterian and Reformed Publishing Company, vol. iii, p.277.
5. F. B. Meyer, *The Way into the Holiest,* Fleming H. Revell Company, p. 104.
6. Frederick S. Leahy, *The Cross He Bore,* The Banner of Truth Trust, pp.9-10.

Chapter 20 — From Gethsemane to Golgotha
1. Hendriksen, *Matthew,* p.957.

On the cross — Introduction
1. Leahy, *The Cross He Bore,* p.65.

Chapter 21 — Christ submitting to the Father
1. Charles Spurgeon, *Metropolitan Tabernacle Pulpit,* vol. xl, p.34.
2. Bunyan, *The Pilgrim's Progress,* p.282.

Chapter 22 — Christ loving sinners
1. William Hendriksen, *New Testament Commentary: Luke,* Baker Book House, p.1028.
2. Spurgeon, *Metropolitan Tabernacle,* vol. xxxviii, p.318.
3. W. Herschel Ford, *Seven Simple Sermons on the Savior's Last Words,* Zondervan Publishing House, p.15.
4. J. C. Ryle, *Expository Thoughts on the Gospels: Luke,* The Baker & Taylor Co., vol. ii, p.476.

Chapter 23 — Christ loving his own
1. Ford, *Seven Simple Sermons,* p.39.
2. F. W. Krummacher, *The Suffering Savior,* Kregel Publications, p.373.

Chapter 24 — Christ peforming the task
1. Hendriksen, *Luke,* p.1034.
2. Thomas Manton, *The Complete Works of Thomas Manton,* Maranatha Publications, vol. ii, p.265.
3. Quoted by A. W. Pink, *The Seven Sayings of the Saviour on the Cross,* Baker Book House, p.79.
4. Hendriksen, *Luke,* p.1034.
5. Pink, *Seven Sayings,* p.74.
6. As above.

Chapter 25 — Christ showing his credentials
1. Ford, *Seven Simple Sermons*, p.58.
2. Bruce Milne, *The Message of John*, Inter-Varsity Press, p.281.
3. Josh McDowell, *Evidence That Demands a Verdict*, Campus Crusade for Christ, Inc., p.166.
4. As above, pp.331-2.

Chapter 26 — Christ finishing the task
1. Edwards, *Works*, vol. i, p.580.

Chapter 27 — The Father satisfied
1. Hendriksen, *Matthew*, p.974.
2. Krummacher, *The Suffering Savior*, pp.411-12.
3. As above, p.413.
4. William Hendriksen, *New Testament Commentary: Romans*, Baker Book House, p.161.
5. Lloyd-Jones, *Romans 3:20 - 4:25*, p.144.
6. Sproul, *Essential Truths*, p.96.

Chapter 28 — Jesus satisfied
1. Walter Chantry, *Psalms for the King of Kings*, The Banner of Truth Trust, p.110.
2. Matthew Henry, *Matthew Henry's Commentary*, Fleming H. Revell Publishing Company, vol iv, p.308.
3. As above.

Chapter 29 — The redeemed satisfied
1. William Hendriksen, *More Than Conquerors*, Baker Book House, p.108.
2. As above.

Chapter 30 — The response of faith
1. Quoted by Hendriksen, *Romans*, p.129.
2. Jim Elliff, *Wasted Faith*, Christian Communicators Worldwide, pp.19-20.
3. Flavel, *Works*, vol. i, p.439.
4. Stott, *Romans*, p.117.
5. Flavel, *Works*, vol. i, p.437.

Chapter 31 — The response of love
1. Hendriksen, *John*, Baker Book House, p.180.

1.
The cross assigned

Titus 1:2; 2 Timothy 1:1,9

Paul's opening words to Titus contain a phrase that is enough to take your breath away. In those words, the apostle is rejoicing in the glorious gift of eternal life. In the midst of his rejoicing, he makes mention of the fact that this gift was promised by God 'before time began' (Titus 1:2).

That is the breathtaking phrase. Stop and think about it. 'Before time began' means before there were any people. So here we have an amazing thing: God made a promise of eternal life for men and women when there were as yet no people to receive it!

The mystery clears when we look at Paul's second letter to Timothy. There he is again talking about this matter of eternal life, and he speaks of '... the promise of life which is in Christ Jesus' (2 Tim. 1:1). A little later he says that the grace of God 'was given to us in Christ Jesus before time began' (2 Tim. 1:9). There is that phrase again — 'before time began'.

The Father's love-gift to the Son

So what we have is this: God made a promise of eternal life for people before there were any people to receive it. But the Second Person of the Trinity, the eternal Son of God, was there when God made the promise of eternal life for people who did not yet exist and, according to Paul, that promise was given to him.

What this amounts to is the Father promising to give the Son a people who would share eternal glory with him. In Ephesians 1:4 the apostle Paul tells us that we were chosen in Christ before the foundation of the world. In Matthew 25:34 the Lord Jesus tells his disciples that a kingdom had been prepared for them from the foundation of the world.

Why would God the Father do such a thing? Why would he give the Son a people for his own? Jesus' prayer in John 17 supplies the answer. There we find him talking to the Father about this very gift, about the people the Father gave him in eternity past. His explanation is this: 'For you loved me before the foundation of the world' (John 17:24).

In his letter to the Colossians, Paul speaks of himself and his readers as being among those whom the Father gave to the Son. He says God 'translated [or "conveyed"] us into the kingdom of the Son of his love' (Col. 1:13). There it is! The Father gave the Son a people because of the love that he had for the Son.

But how did the gift of a people express the Father's love for the Son? There are at least a couple of answers to that. First, in promising these people to his Son, the Father was pledging that they would bring honour and glory to the name of the Son for ever and ever (Eph. 1:12; 1 Peter 2:9-10; Rev. 5:8-14). Secondly, in promising these people to the Son, the Father was pledging that he would eventually make them like the Son (1 John 3:2). It has often been said that the highest form of flattery is imitation. In this case, we might say the greatest way for the Father to express his love for the Son was by making these people like him.

In addition to giving these people to the Son, the Father also wrote their names down in a book — the Book of Life (Revelation 13:8 and 17:8 assert that there is a Book of Life and that it has names in it that were written there before the foundation of the world) — and he promised the Son that he would draw each of these people to him (John 6:37,44).

We may picture it like this. In eternity past, the First Person of the Trinity goes to the Second Person of the Trinity and says, 'As an expression of my love for you, I am going to give you a gift of a people. I am going to draw them to you, and they will serve you for ever, and I am going to make them like you. As much as it is possible for humanity to be like deity, they are going to be like you. They are going to reflect your glory.' That, in effect, is what the Father promised the Son in this inter-trinitarian covenant.

The Son's acceptance of the gift

But there was something for the Son to do in order to receive this love-gift from the Father. This humanity that he was going to receive would have to be redeemed from the ravages of sin. Yes, even before God created Adam and Eve and placed them in the Garden of Eden, he knew they would disobey him and, in so doing, bring the terrible tyranny of sin upon themselves and their descendants.

The people the Father gave to the Son, then, were those whom the Son would redeem from sin. What was necessary for them to be redeemed from sin? God's penalty against sin would have to be paid. That penalty was death, not just physical death (separation of the body from the soul), but rather spiritual death (separation of the soul from God) and eternal death (separation of body and soul from God for ever). That penalty had to be paid! God pronounced it as the just punishment for sin. Had he not demanded that it be carried out, he would have denied his own justice and would have compromised his own character.

To redeem the humanity given to him, the Son had, therefore, to shoulder, or bear, their punishment for their sin. He had
to absorb their death in all its dimensions. In other words,
God's plan of salvation called for the Son to become the surety
for those whom the Father was giving him.

The concept of a surety

A surety is, of course, one who agrees to stand good for
another. He stands as the guarantor for someone else. He
agrees to discharge completely all the obligations of the
person for whom he stands, so much so that the one whom he
represents has no outstanding obligations against him at all.

Now why was it necessary for those who were part of the
Father's love-gift to the Son to have a surety? What would be
their obligations to God, and why would they be unable to
discharge them? As God's creatures, they would be responsible to render perfect obedience to God's law, but they would
fail to do so. Their first surety, Adam, would sin against God
and, in doing so, would bring them into terrible calamity and
ruin.

The only way out of this ruin was for someone else to stand
as their surety. They could not do it themselves. Even if they
could perfectly obey the law of God as their first surety,
Adam, had failed to do, they were already under the sentence
of death.

The Father's plan of redemption called upon his Son to
serve as the surety for those who were his love-gift, to bring
them back into favour with God by doing for them what they
could not do for themselves and by discharging their respon-
sibility. This was the essential ingredient of the Son's acceptance of this gift, and the good news for sinners is that he gladly
and willingly agreed to become the surety for his people.

The work of the surety

This brings us to the very core of the plan of redemption upon which the three persons of the Trinity agreed before the foundation of the world. It can be summarized in three words: 'propitiation through substitution'.

Propitiation. The word 'propitiation' brings us to a reality that is most distasteful and disconcerting to modern ears — namely, the wrath of God. We shall look at this in more detail later, but at this point we must realize that God does not take our sin lightly. He does not smile benignly upon it, or dismiss it as the mere naughtiness of children. He is angry about it. This is a frightening reality, so much so that the psalmist David describes it in these sombre terms:

> God is a just judge,
> And God is angry with the wicked every day.
> If he does not turn back,
> He will sharpen his sword;
> He bends his bow and makes it ready.
> He also prepares for hmself instruments of death;
> He makes his arrows into fiery shafts
>
> (Ps. 7:11-13).

Only if we understand the wrath of God can we delight in that word 'propitiation'. It has to do with wrath being appeased, or satisfied. What a momentous thought! The wrath of God can be appeased. It can be averted so that it does not fall on guilty sinners. This is indeed wonderful news!

Substitution. But exactly how does this happen? The Bible insists that the only way for God's wrath against the sinner to be appeased is for it to fall on a substitute. God's holy character demands that sin be judged. There is no way around this. God cannot just put his wrath away. His justice demands that sin be punished. His wrath must be appeased, and this can be in one of two ways. Either the sinner himself can bear the wrath of God against his sin, or another can come between the sinner and God and endure the stroke of God's wrath in the sinner's place. In other words, there can be a substitute who comes between God and the sinner and absorbs in his own person the wrath of God. God's justice only demands that his sentence against sin be carried out once. So if a substitute comes in and takes on himself the blow of God's wrath, God is completely satisfied.

In order to receive the love-gift the Father was proposing to give him, the Son had to agree to become their substitute. He had to agree to become the Last Adam, to become their representative head and, as such, to take in their place the stroke of God's justice.

How was the Son of God to go about this business of absorbing the punishment of his people in all its dimensions? First, *he would have to come to this world* because this world was the arena, or the realm, in which man would fail. Secondly, *he would have to become a man*. He could not represent his people and pay for their sins unless he was a man himself. The penalty required man to die, and it was only as a man that he could take it on himself.

It was at this point, we might say, that the cross of Christ was erected. This was the type of death God chose for his Son to endure on behalf of the people that the Father was giving to the Son. On that cross, the Son of God would not only experience physical death, but also spiritual and even eternal death.

The redemption of those whom the Father gave to the Son consisted of this — God treated Jesus on the cross as if he had committed every sin ever committed by every person who would ever believe, when, in fact, he had committed none at all. By that death, the Son would satisfy all the demands of God's justice against those people given him by the Father and they would, therefore, be freed from sin and would become his special people.

This redeeming work was what the Father required of the Son in order to receive this love-gift. What was the Son's response to all of this? There is no mystery or uncertainty about it. The Son gladly and willingly accepted the gift of the people and the price of their redemption, and he also pledged that he would not lose any of those whom the Father had given him, but would raise every single one up at the last day (John 6:39-40).

The Holy Spirit's agreement

It is important for us to realize that there was a third party in this council, namely, the Third Person of the Trinity, the Holy Spirit of God.

After the Father gave the Son a people and the Son accepted that gift and agreed to come and provide redemption for them, the Holy Spirit agreed to come after the Son's ascension and apply the benefits of his redemption to their individual hearts.

From the time when God the Father, God the Son and God the Holy Spirit entered into this covenant, the Son set his face towards that cross and began moving towards it. This is the reason why the Bible calls the Lord Jesus Christ 'the Lamb' that was 'foreordained' and 'slain' before the foundation of the world (1 Peter 1:19-20; Rev. 13:8).

How awesome this is! The triune God held a council and we who are redeemed were the subject of it — amazing! The cross was agreed upon there as the means of providing that redemption — astonishing! And each of the three persons of the

Trinity, out of unfathomable love for sinners, followed his part of the plan in perfect faithfulness — incredible! And it was all for guilty sinners!

> From the highest realms of glory,
> To the cross of deepest woe,
> All to ransom guilty captives!
> Flow my praise, for ever flow!
>
> (Author unknown)

2.

The cross needed: man's sin

Genesis 3:1-24

We live in a time when very few people are interested in Christianity. Even many who attend worship services week after week would, if pressed, have to admit that they do not have a vital interest in the things of God. Their church attendance is merely due to force of habit, or a sense of duty, or out of some vague hope of currying favour with God.

Christianity is, of course, about the cross of Christ. Apart from that cross there is no Christianity. So to say people are by and large uninterested in Christianity is to say they are uninterested in the cross. The three persons of the Trinity taking an interest in us and planning the cross is the most astounding thing that can ever enter a mortal mind. But such talk is often met with blankness or boredom these days.

Why is it that so few are vitally interested in the cross of Christ? The answer is not hard to find: they do not see the need of it. There are many things we are not interested in until we see how vital and crucial they are. I am not interested in medicine. I do not normally watch medical reports on television or read medical columns in newspapers. But a few years ago I found myself vitally interested in medicine. A stray tree-branch gave me a skull fracture, and all my apathy about medicine went out of the window. When my personal well-being was at stake my attitude towards medicine changed, and what had formerly been unimportant became very precious to me.

If we are truly to appreciate how vital the cross of Christ is, we must first understand the predicament it was designed to deal with, and to do that we must go back to the beginning.

The crowning-piece of God's creative work was his creation of the first man, Adam, and his wife Eve. The creation of Adam and Eve and the account of their lives together in the Garden of Eden may seem to be a simple story for the entertainment of children, but it involves the most profound truths imaginable, truths that Paul had in mind when he wrote the last half of the fifth chapter of Romans. The account of Adam and Eve in Genesis and the words of the apostle Paul are something like a fabric woven from several threads, or a rope consisting of several strands.

Those strands may be separated and identified as follows: a blessing offered, a test or condition given, a sentence pronounced, the blessing spurned, a principle revealed and a tyranny experienced.

A blessing offered

Consider first the blessing that was offered to Adam and Eve. We find it represented in the book of Genesis by a tree called 'the tree of life' (Gen. 2:9; 3:24).

Adam and Eve probably did not know about it at first. The fruit of that tree, it seems, was to be withheld from them until they had satisfactorily fulfilled a period of probation. Then it was to be given to them and they would enjoy eternal life and full knowledge of God. In addition to that, we may also assume all their posterity would have shared in their victory and received the same benefits. Some mistakenly think Adam and

Eve were not intended to have children until after they fell into sin, but the Bible makes it clear that Adam and Eve were commanded to multiply before sin entered the picture. The only difference made by the Fall was that Eve would now experience pain and difficulty in child-bearing (Gen. 1:27-28; 3:16).

A test given

All that was necessary, then, for man to come into the higher level of existence he was created for, the level at which he would have eternal life and full knowledge of God, was for Adam to obey God faithfully. John Murray puts it like this: 'So a period of obedience successfully completed by Adam would have secured eternal life for all represented by him.'[1]

Adam's obedience to God was reduced to a single test, which is represented in Genesis by another tree, 'the tree of the knowledge of good and evil'. Adam and Eve were told not to eat of the fruit of that tree (Gen. 2:17). All they had to do to secure the blessing represented by the tree of life, then, was to comply with this one condition laid down by God. Perfect obedience to one command would have secured eternal life for them.

What was so wrong about Adam and Eve eating from this particular tree? It was not that the tree itself was evil. It was rather that this tree simply represented the choice God gave them. He could just as easily have told them not to enter a cave, climb a mountain, or cross a river, but he chose to tell them not to eat of the fruit of this tree.

Why was such a test necessary? Adam and Eve were created with a free will, and a free will has to have a choice to make, or it has no meaning or value.

The sentence pronounced

The next thread in this fabric is the sentence that was pronounced. God said that if Adam and Eve ate of the tree which he had told them not to eat of, they would die. They would, in effect, forfeit the privilege of eating of the tree of life and would experience death in three forms — physical, spiritual and eternal. Physical death is the separation of the soul from the body. Spiritual death is the separation of the soul from God. And eternal death is the separation of soul and body from God for ever.

Why would God pass such a severe sentence upon Adam and Eve for failing to live up to this one condition? Why not just give them another chance? After they ate of the forbidden tree, why did God not just say, 'We'll just pretend that never happened, and we'll try again and start from scratch'? God's holiness will not allow him to ignore sin, or pretend it did not happen. For God to do such a thing would be for him to compromise his own character and to deny himself and everything he stands for.

The blessing spurned

Now we come to the next stage, in which Adam and Eve spurned the blessing of eternal life by eating of the tree of knowledge of good and evil. Satan succeeded in getting Eve to eat by persuading her that she would become a god herself in so doing. Eve, in turn, persuaded Adam to eat too.

The tyranny of sin and death

That brings us to the next strand in this complex tapestry — namely, the terrible tyranny of sin and death. At the very moment that Adam disobeyed God by eating of the forbidden fruit, sin and death began to reign in his life. No, he and Eve did not die physically at that very moment. That came much later. But they did die spiritually, and that spiritual death immediately manifested itself in three ways.

The fig-leaf aprons

First, they were immediately conscious of their nakedness and made themselves aprons of fig leaves (Gen. 3:7). What is all this about? Is it merely an indication that Adam and Eve's relationship with each other had changed? There can be no doubt that it had. But the realization that they were naked was primarily an indication that their relationship with God had changed. They now knew they were unfit to stand in his holy presence.

The hiding from God

Another manifestation of spiritual death came when Adam and Eve hid themselves in the garden (Gen. 3:8). Even though they had made themselves aprons, they still had no confidence that they could stand before God. So they ran from him. The fellowship they had enjoyed with God was broken, and they no longer delighted in him and desired to be with him. The word the apostle Paul uses for what Adam and Eve experienced is 'enmity' (Rom. 8:7). They were no longer naturally disposed, or favourably inclined, towards God. They were now afraid of him, suspicious of him and dreaded being in his presence.

The shifting of blame

Still another manifestation of spiritual death can be found in Adam's response when he was confronted with his sin. He immediately shifted the focus to Eve. In so doing, he actually suggested that God himself was responsible for their sin because it was he, after all, who had made Eve. Eve, in turn, shifted the blame to the serpent (Gen. 3:12-13). The inability to see our sin and to confess it openly and honestly is another aspect of spiritual death.

When we stop to consider these manifestations of spiritual death, we find ourselves facing a most gruesome and sickening reality. Adam and Eve were made with minds to comprehend God, hearts to love him and wills to obey him. But all is now dreadfully different. Their minds are darkened with spiritual night so that they are unable to discern the things of God (1 Cor. 2:14; 2 Cor. 4:4). Their hearts are now so degraded that they no longer place their affections on things above, but completely on the things of this earth (Phil. 3:19). And their wills are so deadened that they do not naturally desire God or seek him (Rom. 3:11).

Perhaps the most important question in all of human history is this: how far did man fall? The sobering answer from the pages of Scripture is that he fell as far as he could fall. He is now so tainted by sin that no part of him is free from it. The noble creature made by God is now a depraved, hopeless creature in the mighty grip of a spiritual death that would eventually lead to eternal death.

The principle of representation

The final thread in this story is not to be found in the story of Genesis, but is revealed clearly by the apostle Paul in Romans 5:12-21 — namely, the principle of representation that was at work in all of this. That means Adam was appointed by God as the representative head of the human race, and what he did in this matter of complying with the condition established by

God and being entitled to eat of the tree of life did not count for him alone, but for every single member of the human race. How furious some become at the mere mention of this doctrine! 'It's not fair that Adam should be allowed to act for the whole human race,' they cry. But if we accept the Bible as the Word of God (and there is a mountain of evidence for doing so), we cannot escape this teaching.

There is, however, another dimension to this matter that ought to cause us to hold our tongues — namely, it is through this same principle of representation that we have forgiveness for sins. If one man could not represent others in God's scheme of things, then Christ certainly could not represent his people. They would, therefore, have to bear the eternal consequences of their own sin.

Because of this principle of representation, Adam's act of disobedience caused sin and death to reign tyrannically over the whole human race. Those who refuse to believe we all fell when Adam fell have to explain why we all die. Even babies die before they have the chance to commit a single sin of their own. Why? It is because sin and death are reigning in the human race.

Furthermore, they have to find some way to explain why we all sin. David says of himself: 'Behold, I was brought forth in iniquity, and in sin my mother conceived me' (Ps. 51:5). And what David says of himself in this passage he says of others in another place: 'The wicked are estranged from the womb; they go astray as soon as they are born, speaking lies' (Ps. 58:3).

We can see sin in our *children*. We do not have to teach them to lie, to cheat, to take God's name in vain, to lose their temper, to be selfish, or to show disrespect. They just begin doing these things and a host of others.

We can see sin in *ourselves*. Why do we find it so easy to lie, to lust and to take God's name in vain? Why do we have that desire to tear the reputation of others to shreds? Why are we often so difficult to live with? Why do we find it so hard to do the good things God commands, such as being faithful to attend public worship?

We can see sin in *society*. Murder, violence, sexual promiscuity, lying, stealing, child abuse, corruption in government, abortion, rape, shady business dealings, divorce, war, pornography — these are just a few indicators that something is radically wrong with man, and it is not just a second-rate environment or an inferior education. If a good environment is all that is necessary for people to be good, why are the things we see all around us not restricted to the poor? If a good education is all that is necessary for people to be good, why are these things not restricted to the uneducated?

Simple honesty compels us to admit that the Bible's message is being confirmed every single day. Our world is as it is because men and women come into it with a sinful nature, and that sinful nature is expressed in countless ways.

It is this problem of sin that the cross was designed to deal with. Why did Jesus come? He came because we need a Saviour from this terrible tyranny the Bible calls sin. If it had not been for sin, there would have been no need for him to come, and he would not have come. But because of our sin and because of his grace, he came among us. I have no hesitation in asserting that this is, therefore, the pivotal doctrine in all of Scripture. Everything else hinges on it. The message of Christianity is that we are sinners, but if we are sinners, the sooner we face up to it, the sooner we can receive and rejoice in the solution Christianity offers.

3.
The cross needed:
God's holiness and wrath

Genesis 3:24

Nothing is more mysterious to modern men and women than why God takes sin so seriously. Forgiveness always seems to be the simplest of matters to the sinner. In his eyes it consists of nothing more than God just turning a blind eye and a deaf ear to sin. The sinner can never fathom why God does not just shrug off sin with a casual, 'Forget it.'

What seems so simple to mere men is anything but simple to God. If forgiveness of sin had been a simple matter, God would never have driven Adam and Eve out of the garden of Eden, but would have allowed them to continue living there. By evicting them, God gave overwhelming evidence of how serious a matter sin is.

After expelling Adam and Eve from the garden, Scripture says the Lord God stationed cherubim and a flaming sword at the entrance to Eden (Gen. 3:24). This is not just the author's way of embellishing his story. In those cherubim and in that sword we have the explanation for why God could not regard the sin of Adam and Eve as a trivial, light thing.

The *cherubim* are emblematic of the holy presence of God. We find images of them on the veil and the curtains in the tabernacle, the forerunner of the temple, and then in the temple itself. We find them on the ark of the covenant. The temple was, of course, the place of God's presence, and the ark of the covenant was especially God's dwelling-place (1 Sam. 4:4).

The *flaming sword* must be understood in terms of the righteousness and justice of God that refuses to ignore or excuse sin. It represents the determination of God to punish sin.

The cherubim and the flaming sword present us, then, with the reality of the holiness of God, and that holiness finds its expression in his wrath against sin.

The mere mention of the wrath of God sparks several questions.

Why deal with the wrath of God?

It is considered to be in extremely poor taste even to suggest the wrath of God as a matter for serious consideration. The only time a reference to 'hell' is considered to be appropriate is when it used in profanity. Why, then, would anyone ever dare to speak of the wrath of God in a serious way?

The reason for doing so is that it is in the Bible, and not just in an incidental or occasional way. This teaching is spread evenly across the pages of Scripture. The apostle Paul had much to say about it (Rom.1:18-19; 2:5; 3:5; 4:15; 12:19; Eph. 2:3; 5:6; 1 Thess. 5:9), but we are gravely mistaken if we think this doctrine was his invention. We find it in the preaching of John the Baptist (Matt. 3:12). It is in the book of Hebrews (10:27; 12:25-29) and in the writings of James (James 5:9) and of Simon Peter (1 Peter 4:17-18; 2 Peter 2:4-9). It is in the tiny letter of Jude (Jude 12-15). We find it in the book of Revelation in massive doses (6:16-17; 11:18; 14:10,19; 15:1,7; 16:1,19; 19:15; 20:11-15; 21:8; 22:11,15). And, yes, it is even in the preaching and teaching of the Lord Jesus Christ — very prominently so (Matt. 7:13-14; 22:13-14; 23:33; 25:30,41,46; Mark 9:42-49; Luke 16:19-31; John 3:36).

Some respond to all this by saying, 'I believe in the God of John 3:16.' The wrath of God is there too! We find it right there in the word 'perish' — God so loved the world that he gave his Son so that sinners do not have to perish!

Thank God for the love that sent his Son, but that would have been a very foolish and unnecessary act if there had not been some compelling reason behind it. There would have been absolutely no reason for his Son to come and die had it not been for this dreadful reality of perishing.

What strange times we live in! We want to talk about the Lord Jesus coming to save us while insisting at the same time that there is nothing to be saved from. But there is something to be saved from — it is the wrath of God! And only when we see the terrifying thunderclouds of that wrath do we appreciate the beautiful rainbow of Calvary's love.

There is, then, a vast amount of biblical material on this subject, and no amount of public opinion polls will make it go away.

What is the wrath of God?

It is not, however, enough for us to know that the wrath of God is prominently taught in Scripture. We must know what Scripture says about it. Just what is the wrath of God?

We know what the wrath of man is. Here is a fellow who comes home from work and his wife or children say or do something that does not strike him quite the right way, and he blows up. He stamps his feet, shouts and belittles them. He calls them names and, if he is an even more pathetic specimen of a man, he may actually strike them.

Is God's wrath like this? Not at all. The two types of wrath are entirely different. God's wrath is his settled indignation against our sin. It is not a temporary, emotional outburst of uncontrolled anger. It is, in the words of John R.W. Stott, 'his holy hostility to evil, his refusal to condone it or come to terms with it, his just judgment upon it'.[1] In another place Stott says,

'Our anger tends to be a spasmodic outburst, aroused by pique and seeking revenge; God's is a continuous, settled antagonism, aroused only by evil, and expressed in its condemnation.'[2]

Why does God have wrath?

This drives us to raise yet another question: why does God have such a settled opposition to sin? Why cannot he just ignore it? The cherubim and the flaming sword give us the answer. God's holiness means he cannot be ambivalent, or neutral, about sin. His holiness not only means he must judge sin; it means he has a deep aversion to it. His wrath is kindled against it. In other words, his holiness not only means he must do something about sin, but also that he wants to do something about it. We are often compelled to take a certain course of action that we wish we did not have to take. It is not so with God's action against sin. His very nature is opposed to it. His judgement against sin is, therefore, an expression of his holy nature.

It makes just as much sense to talk about a square circle or a dark light as to talk about God tolerating evil or compromising with it. Every fibre of his holy nature cries out for him to judge evil. His whole being pulsates with indignation against it. One might as well ask the sun not to shine as ask God to ignore evil.

How is God's wrath expressed?

Another question that springs to our minds on this matter of the wrath of God may be stated in this way — how does God express his wrath against sin?

In Romans 1:18 Paul indicates that there is a present, ongoing expression of God's wrath. He says it 'is revealed' from heaven. How is God's wrath being revealed even now?

One way is through conscience. We know certain things are right and other things are wrong. Furthermore, we know wrongdoing should be punished. While we object to the teaching of God's wrath, we cry out for it. Of course, we desire it for others, not for ourselves, and yet all are guilty in the eyes of the holy God.

There are other indications of the present nature of God's wrath. When we see men and women paying a terrible price for their sins in terms of their health, or their family, or their finances, we are seeing the wrath of God being expressed.

A sense of guilt over evil actions is likewise a current expression of God's wrath and, of course, death is another.

Many people would have us believe that God's wrath is completely exhausted by these expressions of it. It is not at all uncommon to hear someone say, 'Our hell is in this life.' But the testimony of the Bible is that these expressions of God's wrath are a warning of a final instalment which Paul calls 'the wrath to come' (1 Thess. 1:10).

The Bible uses an awesome array of terms to describe that final instalment of wrath: hell, the lake of fire, eternal destruction, darkness, weeping and wailing and gnashing of teeth. We do not know the precise nature of this final wrath, but we do know from such terms that it is a reality that is so terrible that it must be avoided at all costs. The resounding cry of Scripture is that it can be avoided. The Lord Jesus Christ died on the cross for the express purpose of delivering all who trust him from the wrath to come.

4.
A survey of Old Testament promises

It is very important for us to realize that there has always been only one way in which sinners can be forgiven and restored to fellowship with God, and that is through his Son, Jesus Christ. The three persons of the Trinity did not agree on the cross in eternity past only to enter into a desperate search for a way to avoid it. From the moment the Son's death on that cross was agreed upon as the means of salvation, the three persons of the Godhead began to move steadily towards it and point towards it. All of the Old Testament must be considered in terms of Christ's unflinching approach to the cross of redemption that he and the Father had agreed upon.

Many fail to understand this. They view the Old Testament in a way that has God frantically trying to find a way of salvation for sinners. They see him, for instance, giving the law of Moses in hopes that the people would keep it and that would be their way of salvation. When all else has failed, God finally sends his Son in one last desperate attempt to save sinners. Such a view not only fails to do justice to Scripture, but it is also terribly derogatory towards God.

Let it be trumpeted clearly: there has always been one way of salvation, and that salvation is in God's Son and his redeeming sacrifice. People in the Old Testament era were saved by looking forward in faith to that sacrifice, and we today are saved by looking backward in faith to that same sacrifice.

Their pointing towards the cross took two forms: promises and types. My purpose in this chapter and the six that follow is to survey these promises and types. In so doing, we shall see that the cross of Christ was not the last, desperate attempt of a reluctant God, but the culmination of his plan from the very beginning.

A survey of the promises of the cross logically falls into three categories: the Law of Moses, the Psalms (or Writings) and the Prophets. This division is forced on us by the Lord Jesus Christ himself. On the evening of the day of his resurrection, he appeared to his disciples in Jerusalem. There he explained his crucifixion and resurrection in these terms: 'All things must be fulfilled which were written in the Law of Moses and the Prophets and the Psalms concerning me' (Luke 24:44).

The Jews recognized a threefold division of the Old Testament books. The Law of Moses was, of course, a general title covering the first five books of the Bible. The 'Prophets' contained some of what we know as the historical books (Joshua - 2 Kings), as well as the writings of the prophets (Isaiah - Malachi). And the Psalms was the designation given to the books of poetry (1 Chronicles - Song of Solomon).

The Lord Jesus Christ insisted that each portion of the Old Testament had to do with him. They were part of his approach to the cross. They foretold it, as indicated above, through both promises and types. We read the Old Testament books correctly, then, only if we look for Christ in them, or only as we read them with a New Testament perspective.

What follows is a brief survey of major promises of the coming of Christ and his work on the cross in each of these major portions of the Old Testament. The next three chapters will be devoted to a more detailed study of one of the promises from each of the major sections of the Old Testament: the books of Moses, the Psalms and the Prophets.

Promises in the books of Moses

This portion of the Old Testament is more rich in types of Christ than in promises, but there are still several promises to be found. The most prominent of these is found in Genesis 3:15. This is followed by the promises God made to Abraham (Gen. 12:1-3; 17:1-7; 22:15-18), to Isaac (Gen. 21:12), to Jacob (Gen. 28:14) and the promise he made through Jacob regarding Judah (Gen. 49:10-12).

Furthermore, we find God making a promise through Moses that the coming Messiah would be a prophet like Moses (Deut. 18:15-19).

One of the most remarkable of the promises God made in this portion of the Old Testament came from the prophet Balaam, the man that stained his calling by harbouring a desire for money. In his prophecy Balaam speaks of a 'Star' that would 'come out of Jacob' and a 'sceptre' that would 'rise out of Israel' (Num. 24:17).

The Bible emphatically affirms that all of these promises were fulfilled by Christ. He was the seed of Abraham (Gal. 3:16), the seed of Isaac (Luke 3:23,34), the seed of Jacob (Luke 3:23,34) and he came from the tribe of Judah (Luke 3:23,33). He is the prophet of whom Moses spoke (Matt. 21:11; Luke 7:16; John 4:19; 6:14; 7:40). And, just as Balaam said, Christ was the bright, shining star that sprang from Jacob (Luke 3:23,34; John 8:12) and the king that rose from Israel (Luke 1:33).

We cannot leave this portion of the Old Testament without a word about the law that God gave to Moses on Mt Sinai. After God delivered the people of Israel from Egypt, he gave them this law. This seems to many to be out of character with everything that God had revealed prior to this about his plan of salvation. Some have even concluded that by giving this law God was opening a new way of salvation and nullifying all he had done before. Nothing could be further from the truth. The giving of the law, far from being a nullification of the promise of redemption through Christ, was in fact an integral part of it.

How can this be? The apostle Paul deals with this matter in his letter to the Galatians. He asks, 'What purpose then does the law serve?' (Gal. 3:19). He then proceeds to answer by saying, 'It was added because of transgressions, till the Seed should come to whom the promise was made... Is the law then against the promises of God? Certainly not! For if there had been a law given which could have given life, truly righteousness would have been by the law. But the Scripture has confined all under sin, that the promise by faith in Jesus Christ might be given to those who believe' (Gal. 3:19,21-22).

The law was given, then, not to be a means of salvation, but to make sinners keenly aware of how desperately they need the salvation Christ would provide on Calvary's cross. It was, therefore, consistent with the promise of salvation through Christ and a further anticipation of it.

Promises in the Psalms

While the other books of poetry contain hints, or glimpses, of Christ, the book of Psalms abounds with promises of his life and work. In its introduction to the Psalms, the Open Bible gives the following list of prophecies and their fulfilment in Christ:

	Prophecy	**Fulfilment**
2:7	God will declare him to be his Son.	Matthew 3:17
8:6	All things will be put under his feet.	Hebrews 2:8
16:10	He will be resurrected from the dead.	Mark 16:6-7
22:1	God will forsake him in his hour of need.	Matthew 27:46
22:7-8	He will be scorned and mocked.	Luke 23:35
22:16	His hands and feet will be pierced.	John 20:25,27
22:18	Others will gamble for his clothes.	Matthew 27:35-36
34:20	Not one of his bones will be broken.	John 19:32-33,36
35:11	He will be accused by false witnesses.	Mark 14:57
35:19	He will be hated without a cause.	John 15:25
40:7-8	He will come to do God's will.	Hebrews 10:7
41:9	He will be betrayed by a friend.	Luke 22:47
45:6	His throne will be for ever.	Hebrews 1:8
68:18	He will ascend to God's right hand.	Mark 16:19
69:9	Zeal for God's house will consume him.	John 2:17
69:21	He will be given vinegar and gall to drink.	Matthew 27:34
109:4	He will pray for his enemies.	Luke 23:34

109:8	His betrayer's office will be fulfilled by another.	Acts 1:20
110:1	His enemies will be made subject to him.	Matthew 22:44
110:4	He will be a priest like Melchizedek.	Hebrews 5:6
118:22	He will be the chief cornerstone.	Matthew 21:42
118:26	He will come in the name of the Lord.[1]	Matthew 21:9

Promises in the Prophets

As we have noted, the Jews' threefold division of the Old Testament placed some of the historical books (Joshua - 2 Kings) in the Prophets. These books were known as 'the former prophets', while the Jews called the books which we refer to as books of prophecy 'the latter prophets'.

The promises of Christ reach their fullest expression in those 'latter prophets'. We might picture it in this way. The promises in the books of Moses are like a spring gurgling up and sending out a stream of water. In the Psalms that little stream gathers strength and force. In the Prophets it is a mighty, rushing torrent.

Nowhere does that torrent rush with more force than in Isaiah's prophecy. He predicts the virgin birth of Christ (7:14), the nature of his work (9:6-7), his lineage (11:1), his anointing with the Holy Spirit (11:2), his forerunner (40:3) and his effect on the Gentiles (60:3).

But the most riveting of all Isaiah's prophecies begins with the thirteenth verse of his 52nd chapter and carries us through chapter 53. There we have the cross of Christ portrayed in such detailed and graphic language that we can practically hear the hammer blows that nailed Christ to the tree. We see the blood flowing down. We hear the angry shouts and taunts of the mob that surrounded the cross. And we marvel that 'By his stripes we are healed' (Isa. 53:5).

While Isaiah is foremost among all the prophets in pointing to Christ, he is certainly not alone. Micah has a startlingly precise prophecy of the birth of Christ (Micah 5:2-5; cf. Matt. 2:1,5-6). Zechariah prophesies his triumphal entry into Jerusalem (Zech. 9:9; cf. Matt. 21:5) as well as his crucifixion (Zech. 12:10; cf. John 19:34). Malachi includes a prophecy about Christ coming to the temple (Mal. 3:1; cf. Matt. 21:12).

It should be noted that these constitute a mere sampling of all the Old Testament promises about the Lord Jesus Christ. A handful would be impressive enough, but there are far more than that. The promises of the Old Testament are so many that we can say they resemble an avalanche.

All of these many promises of the Old Testament are one aspect of the triune God's steady advance towards the cross of Christ.

5.
A promise from the books of Moses

Genesis 3:15

The first of the many Old Testament promises of Christ and his cross was given to Adam and Eve shortly after they disobeyed God.

God would have been perfectly just if he had done nothing except expel them from Eden and leave them to experience the full measure of the consequences of their sin. God could have said, 'I told you plainly, Adam, not to eat of the tree of the knowledge of good and evil. I warned you about the consequences. I gave you plenty of incentives to obey me. I have been good to you in every way imaginable, but you cast it all aside and sinned against me. So now I am going to leave you with the results of your sin.'

Had God done just that and left Adam in his sin, no one could have lifted so much as a single finger of accusation against him. Michael Horton is certainly right to say, 'God would be perfectly just at this point to pull a sheet over the lifeless corpse of humanity.'[1]

It is very important for us to realize this. We shall never appreciate the cross of Christ and the salvation that flows from it until we understand that we did not deserve to be saved and that God was under no obligation to save us.

God could have taken delight in the cherubim and the flaming sword guarding the entrance to paradise. He could have taken pleasure in Adam and Eve being driven away and finally experiencing eternal death. But God did not wash his hands of them and walk away. He could have, but he did not. Before he drove Adam and Eve out of the garden and stationed the cherubim and the flaming sword at its entrance, God announced that plan by which they could be forgiven of their sin and not only restored to fellowship with himself, but restored to paradise itself.

Why did God do it? Why did he make a way of salvation? Some suggest that he saw some good in us despite our sin. This cannot be. Sin left us totally without merit. The reason for God's plan of salvation can never be located by looking at the sinner. It rests entirely in the gracious character of God.

We have seen the holy character of God that demands the punishment of the sinner. But while the holiness of God is very much a part of his character, there is more to be said. God is also gracious and merciful.

Thomas Boston speaks of these two aspects of God's character in this way:

> *Truth* and *Justice* stood up and said, that man had sinned, and therefore man must die, and so called for a condemnation of a sinful, and therefore worthily a cursed creature; or else they must be violated... *Mercy*, on the other side, pleaded for favour, and appeals to the great court in heaven; and there it pleads, saying, 'Wisdom and power, and goodness, have been all manifest in the creation: and anger and justice, have been magnified in man's misery that he is now plunged into by his fall: but I have not yet been manifested. O let favour and compassion be shown towards man, woefully seduced and overthrown by Satan! O!' said they unto God, 'it is a royal thing to relieve the distressed; and the greater anyone is, the more placable and gentle he ought to be.'

But *Justice* replied, 'If I be offended, I must be satisfied and have my right: and therefore I require that man, who hath lost himself by his disobedience, should, for remedy, set obedience against it, and so satisfy the judgement of God.' Therefore the wisdom of God became an umpire, and devised a way to reconcile them.[2]

In Genesis 3:15 we see the grace of God coming to the forefront to announce the plan his wisdom had devised.

Who can measure this grace? It would have been an incredible act of love if God had decided to just take one sinner from Adam's filthy race and clean him up, but — oh, the vastness of God's grace! — he determined, back there in eternity past, to take from Adam's race a multitude of sinners and cleanse all of them — a multitude so vast that the apostle John writes, 'And the number of them was ten thousand times ten thousand, and thousands of thousands...' (Rev. 5:11).

This cleansing work, this redeeming work, was to be done by God's Son, the Second Person of the Trinity, coming to this earth in our humanity and dying on Calvary's cross. That plan, in place before the world began, is now announced for the first time. It is announced to Satan with Adam and Eve standing there in their helplessness and ruin:

And I will put enmity
Between you and the woman,
And between your seed and her Seed;
He shall bruise your head,
And you shall bruise his heel

(Gen. 3:15).

Many claim to have tremendous difficulty in seeing the plan of redemption here, but it is here. The source of redemption is here. The goal or purpose of redemption is here. The means of redemption is here. The certainty of redemption is here. It is all here in God's announcement in the garden of Eden.

The source and the certainty of redemption

The first three words of this announcement, 'And I will...', take us to both the source and the certainty of God's plan of redemption. Those words reflect the total helplessness of Adam and Eve to do anything about the dreadful condition they were in. They had made fig-leaf aprons to cover themselves, but those aprons were totally inadequate to stand in the presence of the holy God.

The willingness of God to redeem

There would have been no hope at all for Adam and Eve had it not been for those words, 'I will'. With those words God indicated his readiness to take up the issue of salvation for his fallen creatures. He did not send Adam and Eve back to the covenant that he had originally made with them, a covenant that theologians have frequently referred to as the 'covenant of works'. The word 'covenant' simply means 'agreement'. God's agreement with Adam and Eve was to bestow eternal life upon them if only they would perfectly obey him. The receiving of this promise depended completely upon what Adam did.

It was obvious after Adam and Eve sinned that a new covenant had to be made. If they could not keep that covenant before they sinned, there was certainly no way they could keep it after they had sinned. And even had they been able to keep the covenant of works from that moment on, something still had to be done about the sin they had already committed. The announcement of Genesis 3:15 signalled the beginning of that new covenant, which can be called 'the covenant of grace'. In this covenant God takes all the covenant obligations upon himself. In respect to Christ, God's covenant was still a covenant of works. He, as the Last Adam, had to undertake and perform all that Adam had failed to do, but in respect to God's people, salvation is entirely a matter of grace. Christ performed all for them even to the point where there is nothing at all left for them to perform. Even the faith by which God's people lay hold of Christ's work is his gift to them (Eph. 2:8-9).

The ability of God to redeem

Not only did God's words to Adam and Eve indicate his willingness to redeem, they also indicated his ability to deal with the problem. We often announce plans that we are unable to carry out. We propose, but we are not always able to dispose. The path of our life is strewn with unfulfilled dreams, aborted plans and shattered hopes.

But what is true of us is not true of God. He is the sovereign ruler of all things. He is unlimited in power and wisdom. What he promises to do, he will do. The God of the Bible is not a frustrated, hand-wringing deity that is fretful or thwarted because he is not able to achieve his will.

The final outcome of redemption will not be a defeated God and a triumphant devil. It will not end with heaven crying in anguish and hell cackling in delight. It will not end with a tearful God disconsolately confessing, 'I tried but failed.'

The purpose of redemption

The purpose of redemption is all wrapped up in that word 'enmity'. If two parties are in a state of enmity, there is no friendship between them. They are not only alienated from each other, but hostile towards each other.

God had made Adam and Eve for friendship with himself, but through their act of disobedience they had alienated themselves from God and formed a friendship with Satan. How dramatically they had fallen — all the way from friendship with God to friendship with Satan!

God was not about to let that friendship stand. His whole purpose in the plan of redemption is to overturn that new friendship. In keeping with that purpose God promises to put enmity between Satan and Eve and between his seed and the Seed of the woman. It essentially amounts to God saying to Satan: 'You have succeeded in forming a friendship with my creatures, but I am going to break that friendship and make them my friends again.'

The means of redemption

God was not content merely to announce his determination to restore friendship between himself and sinful men and women. He also indicated something of the way in which he would do this. It would be accomplished through the incarnation and the crucifixion of the Second Person of the Trinity.

The incarnation of Jesus

Is the incarnation foretold in this first announcement of the plan of redemption? It most certainly is. It is there in God's reference to the 'Seed' of the woman.

In speaking of this Seed, God was promising to send a man. He was essentially saying to Satan, 'You brought sin into the human race through this man Adam. I am now giving you notice that I will provide a way of salvation, a way for sinners to regain paradise, and I will do it through another man.'

Jonathan Edwards says of God's promise: 'In those words of God there was an intimation of another surety to be appointed for man, after the first surety had failed. This was the first revelation of the covenant of grace; the first dawning of the light of the gospel on earth.'[3]

The man God was promising to send would be no ordinary man. He would be 'her Seed', that is, the Seed of the woman. Descent is reckoned through the male, but Christ — the man who is promised by God in these words — did not come from a human father. He was born of the virgin Mary as a result of supernatural conception. He was, therefore, the Seed of the woman. The apostle Paul writes, 'But when the fulness of the time had come, God sent forth his Son, born of a woman...' (Gal. 4:4).

The crucifixion of Jesus

After announcing that this special man was coming, God proceeded to say something very definite about him: he would have to experience severe and painful suffering. This suffering is indicated by these words: 'He shall bruise your head, and you shall bruise his heel.'

God promised that there would be hostility between Satan and this special man, the Lord Jesus Christ. There would be 'enmity' between Satan and all those who belong to him and Christ. This hatred of Satan for Christ was eventually to culminate in his bruising the heel of Christ, but in the process of bruising that heel, Satan would have his own head crushed. There is a significant difference here: the bruising of the heel is very real and painful, but it is not totally devastating. The bruising or crushing of the head is, however, devastating. The head represents authority or dominion.

On the cross the humanity of Christ was bruised, but Satan's kingdom was destroyed. There it would look as if Satan had won a resounding victory. Satan would, as it were, marshal all his forces and succeed in getting evil men to nail Jesus to a cross to die in extreme agony. But what looked to be triumph for Satan would prove to be his undoing. The death of Christ on the cross would actually deal Satan and his kingdom a death-blow because through that death Christ would purchase salvation for his people and open the door for them to regain paradise.

6.
A promise from the Psalms

Psalm 22

It may seem strange to call Psalm 22 a promise, or a prophecy, of the cross of Christ. We think of psalms as hymns of praise, but this psalm is obviously more, much more. Here David lifts up his eyes, looks down the long corridor of time and sees in striking detail the crucifixion of the Messiah.

We have to call this a psalm of prophecy — in the same way that the apostle Peter referred to Psalm 132 as a prophecy (Acts 2:30-31) — because, on the one hand, we can find no experience in David's life that would fit the language he uses in these verses while, on the other, we find that the cross of Christ corresponds to detail after detail of the psalm.

Some have suggested that this prediction of the cross is so exact that it makes us think it had to be written by one who had stood at the foot of the cross. But this is not a psalm by an observer reporting an event. It was written almost a thousand years before the event took place, and it is in the first person. Here we have someone telling about his own experience. We have to say, therefore, that this psalm is the result of the Spirit of God taking over the pen of David in a strange and marvellous way so that he, David, was able to write the very words of the Messiah himself.

The psalm falls into two easily discernible sections. The first is the Messiah's description of the crucifixion (vv. 1-21a). The second is his description of the results of the crucifixion

(vv. 21b-31). We might say the psalm is divided between the Messiah's experience on the cross and his exultation in the results of the cross.

The experience of the Messiah on the cross

The description in these verses leaves us in no doubt that the crucifixion of Christ is in view here.

The words Jesus spoke from the cross

First, some of the words Jesus spoke from the cross are either stated or suggested here. The abrupt opening of the psalm takes us to the very words Jesus spoke when darkness shrouded the land: 'My God, my God, why have you forsaken me?' (Matt. 27:46).

The reference to the speaker's tongue clinging to his jaws (v. 15) makes us think of Jesus' cry, 'I thirst!' (John 19:28).

The very last words of the psalm, which are probably best translated, 'He has done it!' foreshadow Jesus' triumphant cry: 'It is finished!' (John 19:30).

The reason Jesus was on the cross

After the opening cry of this psalm, the psalmist takes us to the reason for it. We find it in in the phrase: 'But you are holy…' (v. 3).

Jesus cried out, 'My God, my God, why have you forsaken me?' for a very simple and obvious reason. He was forsaken by God while he was there on the cross. And why was he forsaken by God? Because he was taking the place of sinners. He was 'made' sin for the love-gift that the Father gave him before the foundation of the world (2 Cor. 5:21). He was bearing their penalty.

The ultimate penalty for sin is to be forsaken by God for ever. It is to be separated from God in that place of eternal destruction called hell (2 Thess. 1:9). In order for Jesus to bear that penalty he had to be forsaken by God.

We have never begun, even in our moments of keenest insight, to understand the depths of Calvary. There the Lord Jesus Christ bore in his own person an eternity of the wrath of God. He, being infinite, suffered in a finite amount of time what we, who are finite, would suffer in an infinite amount of time. Eternity was compressed upon him.

Why did he do it? The holiness of God demanded it. The prophet Habakkuk was right. God is of 'purer eyes than to behold evil' (Hab. 1:13). In that awesome period in which Jesus actually became the sin-bearer, the holy God withdrew from him. God forsaking God — that is the essence and the unfathomable depth of the cross. And it is all clearly foretold in this psalm.

During that time when Christ was forsaken by God, a deep darkness fell over the land (Matt. 27:45). One is tempted to see in the psalmist's phrase 'in the night season' (v. 2) a prophecy of that deep darkness.

The sufferings Jesus endured on the cross

The mockery and ridicule Jesus received are foretold here. The psalmist says:

> But I am a worm, and no man;
> A reproach of men, and despised of the people.
> All those who see me laugh me to scorn;
> They shoot out the lip, they shake the head, saying,
> 'He trusted in the LORD, let him rescue him;
> Let him deliver him, since he delights in him!'
>
> (vv. 6-8).

How exactly this corresponds to what we find in Matthew 27:41-43: 'Likewise the chief priests, also mocking with the scribes and elders, said, "He saved others; himself he cannot save. If he is the King of Israel, let him now come down from the cross, and we will believe him. He trusted in God; let him deliver him now if he will have him; for he said, 'I am the Son of God.'"'

In addition to the mockery, this psalm, as noted above, predicts the thirst of Christ. In his description of the crucifixion, the apostle John notes that this thirst was a fulfilment of prophecy (John 19:28).

We even find the word 'pierced' in this psalm (v. 16), a word that is associated with crucifixion. (The Geneva Study Bible points out that the traditional Hebrew rendering, 'like a lion', which is given as an alternative reading in some versions, probably reflects a copyist's error. The Septuagint, which is the ancient Greek translation of the Old Testament, uses the word 'pierced').[1] The significant point is that David wrote this psalm long before crucifixion was even adopted as a means of execution.

This psalm also prophesies the dividing of Jesus' garments (v. 18) — a prophecy that Matthew notes was minutely fulfilled (Matt. 27:35).

Those who crucified Jesus

Who was it that crucified Jesus? The Roman soldiers? Yes. The Sanhedrin? Yes. But pre-eminently it was God who crucified the Lord Jesus Christ.

Psalm 22 contains hints of the involvement of the Romans (the word 'dogs' in verse 16 was the Jewish way of referring to Gentiles) and the Jews ('the congregation' or 'assembly' of the wicked in verse 16 may very well refer to the Sanhedrin). But the hand of God is not merely hinted at in this psalm; it is explicitly stated in these words, which are addressed to God: 'You have brought me to the dust of death' (v. 15). The precision of this statement is borne out by other Scriptures. The apostle Paul says God 'set forth' his Son as a 'propitiation' for our sins (Rom. 3:25). It was God who refused to spare his Son, but rather 'delivered him up for us all' (Rom. 8:32). It was God who was 'pleased' to 'bruise' the Lord Jesus and 'put him to grief' (Isa. 53:10). Yes, it was God who sent his Son to the cross.

All these things amount to a mere scratching of the surface, but they should convince us that this psalm is indeed saturated with the cross of Christ.

The Messiah's exultation in the results of the cross

Verse 21 brings us to a turning-point in the psalm. The darkness lifts and the sun shines brightly. The storm of wrath has subsided and all is peaceful and calm.

In the verses that remain the Messiah rejoices that his death on the cross was not in vain, but that it has achieved its purpose. Because of that death he now has 'brethren' to whom the name of God can be declared (v. 22). The author of Hebrews relates this portion of the psalm to all those who know the Lord Jesus Christ as their Lord and Saviour. He says Christ is 'not ashamed' to call those who know him his 'brethren' (Heb. 2:10-12).

Furthermore, because of his death on the cross the Messiah rejoices that the poor are able to eat and be satisfied (v. 26). What a marvellous picture this is of sinners coming to know the crucified Redeemer! Because of his death they can eat of the gospel feast and be satisfied with the knowledge that their sins are forgiven and they can, therefore, stand without fear in the presence of the holy God.

The Messiah also rejoices that 'all the ends of the world' shall turn to him (v. 27). His death on the cross was not just for one nation, but for people of all nations, and it will finally issue in the redemption of a multitude 'out of every tribe and tongue and people and nation' (Rev. 5:9).

Yet another cause for rejoicing is the fact that his death will also issue in the final vindication of God. He says, 'And all the families of the nations shall worship before you' (v. 27). This certainly brings to mind the words of the apostle Paul: '... at the name of Jesus every knee should bow, of those in heaven, and of those on earth, and of those under the earth, and that every tongue should confess that Jesus Christ is Lord, to the glory of God the Father' (Phil. 2:10-11).

Finally, he rejoices in the knowledge that 'a posterity' will serve him. There will be in every generation those whom he purchased with his own blood to tell those who come after them of what he has done (vv. 30-31).

So Jesus did not die on the cross hoping that what he was doing would somehow accomplish something. That cross that he and the Father agreed upon before the world began would be effective in redeeming the Father's love-gift. That cross was adopted in eternity past as the only means of salvation. It was announced in Eden and, as Psalm 22 clearly reveals, the Father and the Son never lost sight of that cross throughout the Old Testament period, but ever kept it in view and worked towards its fulfilment.

7.
A promise from the prophets

Isaiah 53

The cross of Christ is promised in the books of Moses and in the Psalms. It is also, of course, promised in the writings of the prophets. Any discussion of the latter must always begin with Isaiah 53. If the promises of the cross to be found in the prophets may be considered in terms of a mountain range, this chapter is Mt Everest. Eight of its twelve verses are quoted in the New Testament in connection with the Lord Jesus Christ (vv. 1,4,5,6,7,8,9,11).[1]

As I have indicated in my book *A Promise is a Promise,* Christ's fulfilment of these prophecies is easily demonstrated:

Consider the following details of Isaiah's prophecy. He says the Messiah would:

be wounded for our transgressions, bruised for our iniquities and receive 'stripes' for our healing (v. 5);
be silent before his accusers (v. 7);
be buried in a rich man's tomb (v. 9);
be innocent of any wrong-doing (v. 9);
be numbered with transgressors (v. 12);
make intercession for transgressors (v. 12).

All of these things would be in keeping with
God's plan: God would smite him (v. 4), lay our
iniquities upon him (v. 6) and bruise him (v. 10).

The writers of the New Testament vigorously assert
and affirm that each one of those seven prophecies
found its fulfilment in Christ.

Peter says the Lord Jesus 'bore our sins in his
own body on the tree' and then specifically quotes
Isaiah's phrase: 'by whose stripes you were
healed' (1 Peter 2:24).
Matthew specifically states that Jesus was silent before his accusers (Matt. 26:63).
Matthew also points out that Jesus was buried
in the tomb of a rich man (Matt. 27:57-60).
Peter asserts that Jesus was innocent of any
wrong-doing, and claims this to be a fulfilment of
Isaiah's words (1 Peter 2:22).
Mark declares that Jesus' crucifixion between
two thieves was a fulfilment of Isaiah's prophecy
that Messiah would be numbered with the transgressors (Mark 15:28).
Luke mentions that Jesus prayed for those who
crucified him, an obvious fulfilment of Isaiah's
claim that the Messiah would make intercession
for transgressors (Luke 23:34).
Jesus himself asserted on numerous occasions
that all he did was in keeping with the plan of God
(John 5:30; 8:42; 18:11).[2]

This much-loved chapter lends itself to a threefold division: the life of Christ (vv. 1-3), his death (vv. 4-10a) and the

results of his death (vv. 10b-12). The major part of it, however, is devoted to his death on the cross.

In dealing with this matter, Isaiah's prophecy sounds many of the same notes as Psalm 22. What Christ was to suffer and why he was to suffer are common to both passages. How Christ was to suffer — that is, with what spirit he suffered — may also be found in both passages, but it is more explicitly stated in Isaiah 53.

What Christ suffered

In his description of the Messiah's death on the cross, Isaiah resorts to a whole catalogue of words that are so keen and graphic they almost make us wince as we read them:

'wounded' (v. 5) — pierced through, deeply and mortally hurt

'bruised' (v. 5) — crushed or broken

'chastisement' (v. 5) — punishment

'stripes' (v. 5) — blows that opened the flesh

'oppressed' (v. 7) — treated harshly and with great hostility

'afflicted' (v. 7) — abused

'taken from prison and judgement' (v. 8) — quickly torn away from due process of law and hastened to death

'cut off' (v. 8) — his life was rudely, violently and abruptly brought to an end

'stricken' (v. 8) — struck violently

In addition the question is posed: 'And who will declare his generation?' (v. 8). The upshot of this question is that no one in his generation — that is, no one among his contemporaries — would speak up in his defence.

The city of Jerusalem suffered extreme hardship when she was invaded by Babylon and her citizens were either killed or deported. The prophet Jeremiah personified that suffering by imagining the city speaking for herself. Here is what she said:

Behold and see
If there is any sorrow like my sorrow,
Which has been brought on me,
Which the LORD has inflicted on me
In the day of his fierce anger

(Lam. 1:12).

Had we been there to see the suffering of Jerusalem at that time, we would certainly have found ourselves in agreement with her. There was no sorrow like her sorrow. That may even have remained true until Jesus came and suffered on the cross, but then it changed. The sorrow and suffering of Jesus on the cross far outstripped that which the city of Jerusalem had experienced. No one has ever suffered what he suffered.

Why Christ suffered

Why did Christ have to suffer such untold agony and anguish on the cross? Isaiah 53 gives us the answer. It tells us that the Christ would not die as others do. His death would have the significance no other death in all of human history would have. It was to be a death for others, a death in which he took the place of others and bore their penalty.

The repeated use of the pronoun 'our' and the preposition 'for' tell us that Jesus would not die for his own sins, but rather for the sins of his people. It was 'our griefs' and 'our sorrows' that he carried with him to the cross. And it was 'for our transgressions', 'for our iniquities' and 'for our peace' that he died (vv. 4-5).

Why was it necessary for him to become the substitute for sinners and die in their stead? It was so they might go free. It all comes down to one thing. If Christ had not died for sinners, those sinners would have to die for themselves. If he had not experienced on the cross an eternity's worth of God's wrath, those for whom he died would have to experience it themselves. But, thank God, he did experience it, and now there is no wrath left for all those who know him. One hymn puts it in these words:

O Christ, what burdens bowed thy head!
Our load was laid on thee;
Thou stoodest in the sinner's stead,
Didst bear all ill for me.
A victim led, thy blood was shed,
Now there's no load for me.

Death and the curse were in our cup:
O Christ, 'twas full for thee!
But thou hast drained the last dark drop,
'Tis empty now for me:
That bitter cup, love drank it up:
Now blessing's draught for me.

Jehovah lifted up his rod;
O Christ, it fell on thee!
Thou wast sore stricken of thy God;
There's not one stroke for me.
Thy tears, thy blood beneath it flowed;
Thy bruising healeth me.

(Author unknown)

Another hymn-writer puts it like this:

Bearing shame and scoffing rude,
In my place condemned he stood,
Seal'd my pardon with his blood;
Hallelujah! what a Saviour!

(Philip Bliss)

We must note that this act of substitution was not something
the Son did in isolation from the Father. The Father and the Son
were not divided over his redeeming work on the cross. The
Lord Jesus did not go there to wring forgiveness out of an
unwilling God. It was God the Father who 'laid' on Jesus 'the
iniquity of us all' (v. 6). It was God the Father who was
'pleased' to 'bruise' him (v. 10). It was God the Father who
'put him to grief' (v. 10) and who would 'make his soul an
offering for sin' (v. 10).

It is also crucial for us to realize that the only way Jesus
could become the substitute for others was if he had no sins of
his own. If Christ had been guilty of so much as a single sin,
he would have had to pay for his own sin and could not,
therefore, have paid for the sins of others. Even this dimension
of Christ's atoning death is not excluded from Isaiah's prophecy. He says of Christ: 'He had done no violence, nor was any
deceit in his mouth' (v. 9).

How Christ suffered

Isaiah's amazingly detailed description of the cross does not
end with what and why the Christ would suffer. It also unfolds
the spirit with which he would suffer. Isaiah puts it in these
words:

He was oppressed and he was afflicted,
Yet he opened not his mouth;
He was led as a lamb to the slaughter,
And as a sheep before its shearers is silent,
So he opened not his mouth

(v. 7).

Christ went to the cross, not with a grudging obedience that could not find any way to escape it, but with a glad and ready willingness. During his public ministry he constantly emphasized that he had come to do the Father's will, and that will carried him all the way to the cross. Even when the cross was only a few hours away, he was able to say to the Father: 'Your will be done' (Matt. 26:42).

The lamb before its shearers is indeed a most appropriate emblem for the willingness of Jesus to go to the cross. The lamb does not intimidate and frighten. It does not roar like a lion, or strike rapidly like a snake. It is not able to sink its teeth deep into its enemies. It is completely defenceless against those who would harm it.

When Jesus stood before those who wanted to take his life, he did so like a lamb. A lamb has no choice about being a lamb, but Jesus had a choice. He, as the eternal Son of God, could have called for 'more than twelve legions of angels' to utterly obliterate those who wanted to crucify him (Matt. 26:53), but he chose to be like a lamb and passively submit to the sufferings of the cross. How thankful we should be for that submission! Without it there would have been no way for us to escape the wrath of God.

It is noteworthy that all that Isaiah says by way of describing the cross is couched in the past tense. In other words, he speaks of it as though it had already taken place, even though he lived more than seven hundred years before Christ. There is only one way to explain this. The Spirit of God had so drilled into Isaiah's spirit the certainty of that coming cross that the prophet could speak of it as though it were already accomplished.

That cross was made certain by the covenant of the Father, the Son and the Spirit, and Isaiah 53 marks another of their steady, determined steps towards it.

8.
The cross typified:
the institution of sacrifice

Leviticus 16

After Adam and Eve sinned, God pointed them to his plan of redemption in two ways. First, he gave them a promise (Gen. 3:15). Secondly, he gave them a type.

The promises and types of the Old Testament are the ways in which God kept his people looking towards the coming Redeemer. We have traced the stream of promises through the Old Testament by surveying the most prominent among them and by going into detail about three in particular. Now we pick up the other means by which God pointed to the coming Redeemer, that is, through types.

A type is a picture, or an emblem, of redemption. It is something that captures and expresses the very essence of redemption. It may be an institution, an event, or a person. In this chapter we look at the institution of sacrifice. In the next two chapters, we shall look at an event and a person that typified the work of Christ.

While there are many such types of Christ's redeeming work in the Old Testament, it is safe to say that the greatest of all these types is the institution of the sacrifice of animals.

The first instance of sacrifice

The first such sacrifice took place there in the garden of Eden before God drove out Adam and Eve (Gen. 3:21). The sacrifice of those animals brings us to the very essence, or core, of God's plan of redemption, which is, as we have established, propitiation through substitution.

The only way for sinners to be forgiven is for God's anger against them to be appeased. And the only way for it to be appeased is for the sinner to be punished or judged. Now here is where the element of substitution comes in. If someone else comes in between the sinner and God, that substitute bears the punishment, or the judgement of God. God is, therefore, satisfied because sin has been punished but, at the same time, the sinner is spared because the punishment of God has fallen on another.

In the case of Adam and Eve, we may picture it in this way: the wrath of God was going out towards them because of their sin, but before it could fall upon them, a substitute came between them and God, and the wrath fell upon that substitute. That substitute is pictured by God's slaying animals and using their skins to clothe Adam and Eve. This signified at one and the same time that the works of their own hands, their fig-leaf aprons, were not sufficient for them to stand acceptably in his presence, and that they could stand acceptably before him on the basis of his wrath being propitiated by its being spent on a substitute.

From this starting-point, the practice of substitution becomes central to the Old Testament. Every time we see an animal being sacrificed we see this principle of substitution at work. The Geneva Study Bible says, 'In every animal offering the worshipper placed his hand on the victim's head, thereby identifying himself with the animal, saying in effect, "This animal represents me." The animal sacrifices involved the animal's death, and so the sacrifices had atoning symbolism: the animal dying in the sinful worshipper's place represented redemption from the death he deserved.'[1]

When we say something is a type of Christ, we do not necessarily assert that those people who were personally and directly involved in the action or event recognized it as such. God sees the end from the beginning. He sees his people in every age, and some of the types he gave in the Old Testament were designed so that those saints who came along after Christ could have their faith confirmed and strengthened by looking back into the Old Testament and seeing their Lord there.

But this greatest of all the types, the sacrifice of animals, was most certainly intended to point the people who practised it to Christ. Thomas Boston writes of these sacrifices, 'I say, there is no question but every spiritual believing Jew, when he brought his sacrifice to be offered, and according to the Lord's command laid his hands upon it, whilst it was yet alive ... he did from his heart acknowledge that he himself had deserved to die; but by the mercy of God he was saved, and his desert laid upon the beast; and as that beast was to die, and be offered in sacrifice for him, so did he believe that the Messiah should come and die for him, upon whom he put his hands, that is, laid all his iniquities by the hand of faith.'[2]

It should be obvious to us that these animals had no power in themselves actually to make atonement for sin, but they could point to the coming of the perfect substitute, the Lord Jesus Christ. The plan of God required his Son to become the substitute for his people — that is, to die in their stead. Whenever, therefore, we find this principle of substitution, one dying in the place of another, we have a picture, or anticipation, of the cross of Christ.

Further instances of sacrifice

Cain and Abel

This matter of substitution is the focus of the story of Cain and Abel (Gen. 4:1-8). We may rest assured that Adam and Eve carefully informed their sons of the need to approach God through the shedding of the blood of innocent animals. Abel accepted this word and brought an animal sacrifice to God. Cain, on the other hand, having heard the same message, refused to come in the way God had commanded. Instead he brought the works of his own hands — that is, the fruit of the ground. Henry Mahan says of Cain's offering: 'It was a bloodless sacrifice, thereby denying his need of the Redeemer, the Lord Jesus Christ. Cain would be his own priest, his own mediator and his own intercessor... It denied that he was a sinner before God, who deserved condemnation and death. He approached God on the grounds of his own merit and works.'[3]

Abraham and Isaac

Substitution was also the focus when Abraham took Isaac up the mountain to offer him up as a burnt offering (Gen. 22:1-14). Isaac was spared because God gave Abraham a ram to offer in his stead, and Abraham came down from that mountain looking forward to the coming Christ and saying, 'In the Mount of the LORD it shall be provided' (Gen. 22:14).

The Passover

Substitution was the issue when the children of Israel were in bondage in Egypt. God announced that he was going to send his angel of death through the land and that those who would escape the sentence of death must slay an unblemished lamb and place its blood at the top and at the sides of their doors. And the promise he gave was this: 'And when I see the blood, I will pass over you' (Exod. 12:13).

The greatest instance of sacrifice

The whole sacrificial system God instituted for the people of Israel was built on the concept of substitution. Martyn Lloyd-Jones writes, 'The blood always means the life poured out. So that in the animal sacrifices the blood means that the animal had been put to death, the life had been taken, and the blood was taken as proof positive of that — that the animal had suffered death. The punishment that should have come upon the Jews had come upon the animal as the substitute. The blood was presented in order to prove the fact of death. "Blood" means therefore "a sacrificial death".'[4]

In the seventh month of the Hebrew calendar (our October) came the most important day of the year for the people of Israel. It was the day in which atonement was made by the high priest of the nation for the sins of the people (Lev. 16:1-34).

The procedure

The high priest of Israel was to follow carefully a clearly defined procedure:

>   1. He was to wash himself thoroughly and dress in linen (v. 4).
>   2. He was to bring to the tabernacle a bull as a sin offering for himself and his family and a ram as a burnt offering (v. 3).

3. He was to take two goats to the tent of meeting and by lot select one to be a sacrifice and the other to be used as a scapegoat (vv. 7-10).

4. He was to sacrifice the bull as an offering for himself and his family, and take its blood, along with a censer of burning coals and some fine incense, into the Most Holy Place. There the blood was to be sprinkled on the mercy-seat. This sprinkling was to be done seven times with his finger (vv. 11-14).

5. The goat selected for sacrifice was to be slain as an offering for the sins of the people. Its blood was also to be sprinkled on the mercy-seat (vv. 15-16).

6. The high priest was to sprinkle the blood of the goat in the tabernacle of meeting (v. 16) and on the main altar (vv. 18-19).

7. The high priest was then to lay his hands on the head of the second goat, confess the sins of the people and send the goat into the wilderness (vv. 20-22).

8. After this the high priest was to remove his linen garments, wash himself, dress in his regular garments and offer burnt offerings for himself and for the people (vv. 23-24).

9. The skins and flesh of the animals used for sacrifice were to be taken outside the camp and burned (v. 27).

We should also note that the high priest alone was to do all these things and that no one was to be near him when he did them.

The central truth

Such a procedure seems very strange these days, and many are inclined to see it as a custom devised by a very primitive and superstitious people. But it was something far greater than that. Indeed, this procedure was not devised by the people of Israel at all; it was given to them by God as an affirmation on a much larger scale of the same truth announced in Eden — namely, that guilty sinners can be acceptable to God on the basis of a substitute who bears their penalty. The word 'atonement' itself suggests substitution. To make 'atonement' means 'to cover over'. The death of the animals in place of the sinner 'covers over' the sin of the sinner and, in so doing, shields him from the wrath of God.

It must always be remembered, however, that the animals sacrificed could not in reality take the place of sinners. An animal cannot pay for a man's sin (Heb. 10:4). But those animals could and did serve the purpose of pointing forward to the one who could indeed be a substitute for sinners, the Lord Jesus Christ. Because he was a man, he could take the place of men. Because he was the God-man, he could take the place of more than one man. The Day of Atonement must be seen, therefore, as an additional picture of the work of Jesus Christ, the perfect substitute.

When we approach that day with Christ in mind, we are immediately able to see some important distinctions and some very interesting parallels.

Important distinctions

One of these distinctions is that on the Day of Atonement the high priest offered the blood of another — and an involuntary victim at that — in the Most Holy Place. But the Lord Jesus Christ is both our High Priest and our sacrifice. In other words, he, as High Priest, offered his own blood as the sacrifice for his people, and he did it voluntarily.

A second distinction should go without saying: while the high priest of Israel had to first make atonement for himself, the Lord Jesus, as our High Priest, had no sin for which to atone. He was, in the words of the apostle Peter, 'without blemish and without spot' (1 Peter 1:19).

Another important distinction is that while the high priest of Israel had to make atonement for the sins of the people on a yearly basis, which signified the inability of the animals to atone for the sins of men, the Lord Jesus Christ atoned for the sins of his people once and for all (Heb. 9:25-28).

> Not all the blood of beasts,
> On Jewish altars slain,
> Could give the guilty conscience peace,
> Or wash away the stain.
>
> But Christ, the heavenly Lamb,
> Takes all our sins away;
> A sacrifice of nobler name,
> And richer blood than they.
>
> (Isaac Watts)

In addition to these things, we must observe that on the Day of Atonement the high priest went into an earthly sanctuary to offer up his sacrifices. The Lord Jesus Christ, however, went into the heavenly sanctuary (of which the earthly sanctuary was a mere copy) to make his atonement (Heb. 9:11-15,23-24). This does not mean the Lord Jesus Christ actually carried his shed blood into heaven itself, but rather that he entered into heaven as our High Priest on the basis of, or by virtue of, his shed blood.

Finally, the high priest of Israel went into the Most Holy Place as the representative of his people. No one was allowed to follow him there. But Jesus Christ is not only the representative of his people, but also their forerunner (Heb. 6:20). In other words, he has, as their High Priest, made it possible for them to follow him into heaven itself.

Interesting parallels

The following are some of the major ways in which the work of Christ is pictured, or typified, by the Day of Atonement.

Firstly, the high priest's actions in putting off his regular garments, washing himself and putting on white linen may be taken as a picture of Christ laying aside his glory and being clothed in our humanity, a humanity in which he was undefiled by sin (Heb. 7:26).

Secondly, the two goats, one for the sin offering and the other as the scapegoat, must be taken as a type of two aspects of the work of Christ. He not only died as our sin offering but, in doing so, also bore our sins away to such a degree that they will never be found again or remembered again (Heb. 8:12).

Thirdly, the fact that the high priest alone performed all the work on the Day of Atonement pictures the truth that Christ alone made atonement for his people. Christ is truly able to take up the words of the prophet Isaiah: 'I have trodden the winepress alone, and from the peoples no one was with me' (Isa. 63:3).

Fourthly, as the burning of the skins and flesh of the animals used for sacrifice on the Day of Atonement was to take place outside the camp, so Christ went outside the city of Jerusalem to be consumed with the fire of God's wrath (Heb. 13:11-12).

Finally, one of the most interesting aspects of the Day of Atonement has to do with the ark of the covenant and the mercy-seat. The ark contained the tables of stone on which God had written the Ten Commandments. Those tables represented the righteous demands of God. The mercy-seat was set above the ark, and was exactly the same width as the ark. When the high priest sprinkled the blood of the sacrifice on the ark, it indicated that the blood of that innocent substitute perfectly satisfied the demands of God's law. That constitutes a beautiful picture of the cross of Christ. There Jesus shed his blood and perfectly satisfied God's demand for sinners to be punished for their sins. The law of God is perfectly answered by the cross of Christ.

The purpose of the Day of Atonement, then, was to point the people to the atonement of the Lord Jesus Christ. Each year it reminded the people of the plan of redemption God announced to Adam and Eve, a redemption that was made possible only by the coming Christ offering himself up as the substitute for them.

9.
The cross typified:
a significant event

Genesis 6:11 - 7:24

The sacrifice of animals was instituted by God himself for the express purpose of typifying, or picturing, the redeeming work of the coming Christ. It must, therefore, be considered the most significant of all the Old Testament types. Furthermore, by its very nature it most closely resembled the work Christ would actually perform. But there are other types of Christ's saving work as well. These types may be divided into two categories: events and persons.

Some think it is only legitimate to consider something a type of Christ if a New Testament passage expressly affirms it to be such. While it is possible to fall into the trap of type-mania, it is also safe to say there are some events and persons that so obviously embody the core truths of the gospel that they are meant to be considered as types. One of the Old Testament events of this nature is the ark of Noah (Gen. 6:11 - 7:24). The biblical account compels us to recognize a couple of major parallels.

Two kinds of rain

The rain of Noah's day

The rain that fell upon Noah's generation was no ordinary rain. That may seem to be one of the most notable understatements of all time. Of course it was no ordinary rain! Some think there had been no rain prior to this, but that the earth was watered by 'a mist' that 'went up from the earth and watered the whole face of the ground' (Gen. 2:6). If that was the case, the very fact that it rained at all was extraordinary.

But the extraordinariness of the event did not end there. It rained and rained, even to the point where Scripture says, 'The windows of heaven were opened.' In addition to that the account tells us, 'All the fountains of the great deep were broken up' (Gen. 7:11). This leads us to believe that vast reservoirs of water under the surface of the earth erupted. The outcome of it all is stated in these terse words: 'And the waters prevailed exceedingly on the earth, and all the high hills under the whole heaven were covered' (Gen. 7:19).

It was no ordinary rain; that is certain. But, having said all that, we still have not arrived at the one crucial factor that made this no ordinary rain. This rain was not just a freak natural event. It was not just nature going berserk. To get to the bottom of this flood of water, we have to say it was a rain of God's wrath. It came upon Noah's generation because of their callous disregard for God's laws.

Scripture is explicit about this matter. It tells us these people were 'corrupt' and violent (Gen. 6:11-12). The Lord Jesus himself had this to say about that generation: 'They ate, they drank, they married wives, they were given in marriage, until the day that Noah entered the ark, and the flood came and destroyed them all' (Luke 17:27).

No, they did not come under the wrath of God just for eating, drinking and marrying. There is nothing wrong with these things in themselves. But there is something wrong when people begin to live so much for them that they have no regard at all for God and his laws. And that is exactly what the people of Noah's day were doing. They went blissfully along their way as if there were no God and no eternity.

God gave them ample opportunity to repent. While Noah was building the ark, he was also warning his neighbours about the wrath to come (2 Peter 2:5), but they dismissed him and his preaching and continued their love affair with iniquity.

The rain that fell upon Noah's generation was, then, a rain of wrath.

The rain of wrath that we face

Just as Noah's generation faced a rain of wrath, so do we. No, it is not the same type of rain that Noah's day faced. It is not water falling from the sky and bursting up from beneath the earth. The Bible speaks of it rather as a rain of fire. David says of the Lord: 'Upon the wicked he will rain coals; fire and brimstone and a burning wind' (Ps. 11:6).

Untold numbers have not learned from the rain of wrath on Noah's generation, and they are living just as those people did. They are living as if this world is all there is, or all that matters — as if God has died, or never existed at all. They hear about the commandments of God, but they are so absorbed with their own pursuits that they have no interest in those commandments.

All parents know something of how they would respond if their children, after receiving all manner of benefits from them, were to live with total disregard for their values. Multiply that by infinity and you can begin to understand how God feels about his creatures living without regard for his commandments after he has bestowed all manner of benefits upon them.

All those who live this way are destined to experience the flood of God's wrath. That wrath, even now evidencing itself in various ways (Rom. 1:18), will finally be complete in a place of eternal destruction away 'from the presence of the Lord and from the glory of his power' (2 Thess. 1:9).

Two arks

The account of Noah brings before us, then, the grim reality of the wrath of God. But, thank God, that is not all it teaches us. Noah's experience allows us to talk about two arks.

Noah's ark

When God told Noah about the impending flood of wrath, he also commanded him to build an ark according to certain specifications (Gen. 6:14-16). After years of hard work, the ark was finally completed and, just as God had said it would, the rain began to fall. That rain of his wrath fell and went on falling. But because of the ark that rain, while it fell on everyone else, did not fall on Noah and his family. They were in the ark, and the rain fell on the ark and not on them.

Christ as our ark

Noah's ark provides us with a remarkable picture of the ark that God has made available to sinners. That ark has a name — the Lord Jesus Christ.

All of us are sinners by nature, and by virtue of our sins we are facing this terrific storm of the wrath of God. But the situation is not hopeless. Jesus Christ, God's Son, took unto himself our humanity, and in that humanity went to die on the cross. Do you wonder what the cross is all about? On that cross Jesus took God's wrath in the place of guilty sinners. Just as the rain of wrath fell on the ark in Noah's day, so the wrath of God fell on Jesus there on the cross.

And because that wrath fell on Jesus, the good news of the gospel is this — not one drop of wrath will ever fall on those who are in Jesus. This is why the apostle Paul is able to assert triumphantly: 'There is therefore now no condemnation to those who are in Christ Jesus' (Rom. 8:1).

When it comes to this matter of the wrath of God, there are only two positions: that wrath is either upon us, or it is upon Christ. If God finds our sin upon us, he will send his wrath to fall on us; but if he finds our sin upon Christ, his wrath against us will be averted.

That brings us back to the word 'propitiation'. That word conjures up this image. Here is wrath coming out from God and heading towards the sinner, but before it falls upon the sinner, someone steps between God and the sinner and absorbs the wrath.

Jesus Christ is the propitiation. He is the only safe refuge in the storm of God's wrath. Let the rain of wrath fall. Let the tide of judgement swell ever so high. All who are in Christ are safe.

10.
The cross of Christ typified:
a significant person

We find the saving work of Christ typified in the Old Testament, not only by the institution of sacrifice and by remarkable events (the flood of Noah is only one among many), but also by several people.

Joseph is one such example. He, as the kinsman of his family, saved them from famine even though they originally had an evil disposition towards him. In like manner, Christ, who became our kinsman by taking our humanity, saves his people from spiritual ruin even though they originally hated him. We can go further and say that just as Joseph was willing to endure incredible humiliation in order to save his people temporally, so Christ was willing to endure humiliation in order to save his people eternally.

Moses, who was called by God to lead his people from slavery in Egypt to the land of Canaan, wonderfully pictures Christ leading his people from the slavery of sin to eternal rest in heaven.

The most significant of all these personal types, however, is David. The connection between him and the Lord Jesus is truly amazing. It is so strong that God announced the coming of Christ to Ezekiel in these terms: 'I will establish one shepherd over them, and he shall feed them — my servant David. He shall feed them and be their shepherd. And I, the

LORD, will be their God, and my servant David a prince among them; I, the LORD, have spoken' (Ezek. 34:23-24).

When we come to the New Testament we find the Lord Jesus referred to as 'the seed of David' (John 7:42; Rom. 1:3; 2 Tim. 2:8), 'the son of David' (Matt. 9:27; 15:22; 20:30; 21:9,15; Mark 10:47; Luke 18:38; 20:41), 'the Root of David' (Rev. 5:5) and 'the Root and the Offspring of David' (Rev. 22:16). Furthermore, when Gabriel announced the conception of Jesus to Mary he included this phrase: 'The Lord God will give him the throne of his father David' (Luke 1:32).

Some of the connections between David and Christ are immediately obvious. David's home town was Bethlehem, and Jesus was also born there. In his early years David was a shepherd, caring for his father's sheep, and Jesus is the Shepherd of the flock given to him by his Father (John 10:14-18). David was plucked from obscurity and anointed as king over Israel, and Jesus spent his early years in obscurity in Nazareth. When David was anointed, the Spirit of the Lord came upon him (1 Sam 16:13), and at his baptism the Lord Jesus was anointed with the Spirit of God (Matt. 3:16).

Such a list of parallels could go on and on, but we should focus on those portions of the life of David which most graphically portray the saving work of Christ on the cross.

David slays Goliath

Few today, it seems, see the much-loved story of David and Goliath (1 Sam. 17) as a picture of the cross of Christ. It has come to be regarded as something of a summary for dealing with the various problems of life. These problems become Goliath, and those who are trying to deal with them David. Then the question is raised: how did David defeat Goliath? Why, it was with his sling and five smooth stones. And that

sling and those smooth stones suddenly become the resources
that we have for coping with the problems of life. David
obviously had faith in God, so that becomes one of the stones
we can use in defeating the giants of life. David must surely
have been a man of prayer. So that becomes another stone.
David evidenced determination, a quality we must obviously
have to handle the problems of life. And so it goes on. The
popular treatment of David and Goliath is, then, that we can
easily defeat the problems we face in our lives, no matter how
intimidating they may be, by summoning all the resources God
has placed at our disposal.

While there may be a grain or two of truth in such an
approach, it completely misses the remarkably glorious picture of the gospel of Christ, the main message Scripture is
concerned to convey. Where is the gospel in the story of David
and Goliath? If we think of David as the representative of his
people going out to slay the giant with the unlikely instrument
of a sling, we have a moving picture of Christ, as the representative of his people, taking the unlikely instrument of a
Roman cross and dealing the death-blow to Satan and his
kingdom. By virtue of that act Christ delivers his people just
as David, by slaying Goliath, delivered Israel.

David flees from Saul

We might have expected that David's heroic deliverance of
the people from Goliath and the Philistines would have earned
Saul's undying gratitude. Instead it kindled in him seething
jealousy and resentment and murderous rage (1 Sam. 18-26).
Saul hated David for no reason.

Even in the face of extreme provocation, David refused to
respond in kind. When he had opportunities to take Saul's life,
he spared him. All the time that he was persecuted and pursued

by Saul, David remained faithful to his king and his nation. This part of David's life captures another aspect of Christ's redeeming work. Not only was he also hated without a cause (Ps. 69:4), but he remained faithful and true to the work the Father had sent him to do.

We can go even further. It was God who preserved David from all the machinations and schemes of Saul, even when it appeared as if there was no way for David to escape. And it was the same God who protected and preserved the Lord Jesus Christ from the evil schemes of those who wanted to kill him. God's protection of David amounted to protection of the plan of redemption, of which God had chosen David to be a vital part. And God's protection of Jesus was for the same purpose. Jesus could not die one day before the time the Father had appointed.

David rules as king

At no point in his life does David shine more brightly as a type of Christ than during his glorious reign over the people of God. During this time God's people enjoyed abundant blessing from their God. Their enemies were subdued. Their worship was greatly enriched as a steady stream of psalms flowed from David's pen. And David himself received glorious promises from God. All of these portray the kingly work of the Lord Jesus Christ.

Enemies subdued (2 Sam. 5:6-9)

One of David's most impressive victories was the conquest of the city of Jerusalem. Jonathan Edwards says the city of Jerusalem was 'the greatest type of the church of Christ in all the Old Testament. It was redeemed by David, the captain of the hosts of Israel out of the hands of the Jebusites, to be God's holy city, the holy place of his rest for ever, where he would dwell.'[1]

Then Edwards applies this to Christ in these words: 'So Christ, the Captain of his people's salvation, redeems his church out of the hands of devils, to be his holy and beloved city. And therefore how often does the Scripture, when speaking of Christ's redemption of his church, call it by the names of Zion and Jerusalem!'[2]

Mercy granted to the helpless (2 Sam. 9:1-8)

One of the prerogatives of a king is to grant mercy to various ones. The most striking example of this in the life of David is the case of Mephibosheth. The grandson of Saul and the son of Jonathan, this man was in a most miserable and wretched condition. He had no inheritance and was completely unable to do anything about his situation because he was crippled.

Even though Mephibosheth had no hold on David at all and no right to expect anything from him, David showed him mercy. Acting on the basis of the covenant he had with Mephibosheth's father (1 Sam. 20:15), David compelled Mephibosheth to come to him (v. 5). He calmed his fears, restored to him all that he had lost and guaranteed personal fellowship between the two of them (v. 7). Mephibosheth gladly accepted David's offer, acknowledging his own terrible condition and with profound humility and gratitude (v. 8).

All of this constitutes a moving picture of the sovereign Christ extending mercy to sinners who, like Mephibosheth, have lost all through sin and are completely unable to help themselves. Even though there is nothing about sinners to commend them to Christ, he delights in calling them to himself, calming their fears, restoring to them what they have lost and assuring them that they have been brought into a state of fellowship with him.

God's people enriched (2 Sam. 23:1-2)

As he approached the end of his life, David reflected on the many blessings that God had bestowed upon him. One of the chief of those blessings was that God had made him 'the sweet psalmist of Israel'.

It is interesting to note that David saw his role as psalmist in terms of the people of Israel. He was not a psalmist for his own enjoyment, although we may be sure he derived substantial delight from his psalms. Instead he saw his psalms as a means of blessing for the nation. Those psalms did not come as a result of his own ingenuity or creativity. David explains them in this way: 'The Spirit of the LORD spoke by me, and his word was on my tongue' (2 Sam. 23:2). He was the channel through which God enriched and blessed the people.

As the King of his people, the Lord Jesus Christ has ascended on high to the Father and given gifts to men (Eph. 4:7-12). The single greatest gift came on the Day of Pentecost. The apostle Peter explained that day in terms of the ascended Lord pouring out upon his people the gift of the Holy Spirit in accordance with the promise he had received from the Father (Acts 2:33).

The gifts of the ascended Lord to his people are such that the apostle Paul was able to say to the Corinthians, 'I thank my God always concerning you for the grace of God which was given to you by Christ Jesus, that you were enriched in everything by him in all utterance and all knowledge...' (1 Cor. 1:4-5).

David receives God's promise (2 Sam. 23:5)

When David received from God the promise that his kingdom would be established for ever, the work of the Lord Jesus Christ was anticipated in two ways.

First, the promise was fulfilled by Christ. Because he is the ever-living one, Christ, the seed of David, guarantees that David's kingdom will be permanent.

Secondly, we also have here a picture of the promise that Christ himself has received from God the Father — the promise of an everlasting kingdom. This covenant was made by the Father with the Son even before the world began. It is 'ordered' — that is, it is all carefully planned and arranged by God. Nothing is left to chance. It is also 'secure'. It rests on the unchanging God who is faithful to do all that he promises to do.

We must also remember that it is to Christ, and Christ alone, that all the promises of God are made. He, as the covenant head of his people, receives them from God the Father and, in turn, showers them upon his people.

By virtue of his saving work on the cross, the Lord Jesus Christ has received the promise of an everlasting kingdom from his Father (Heb. 1:8-13) and, through him, all his people receive that promise as well.

David as a type of Christ — a summary

The above instances are just a few in which David can be seen to be a personal type of Christ. And the fact that the Bible gives so much attention to David tells us that God was using him to point to the coming Messiah and his work on the cross. This constitutes further confirmation that the work of Christ is the grand, unifying theme of the Scriptures.

It is important for us to realize that no type of Christ is perfect in every respect. Types can at best give only a faint portrayal of the glory and perfections that are his. Nowhere is this more obvious than in the life of David. At his very best, David was nothing more than a sinful man who was capable of great evil. The account of his sordid affair with Bathsheba and his deliberate murder of Uriah is a sad commentary on the reality of sin even in the life of a child of God.

How, in the light of the terrible things David did, can we claim him as a type of Christ? Such sin does not, of course, typify Christ, who was sinless in every respect. But it does underscore for us the need for Christ, the truly righteous King who, by his redeeming work, provides an incorruptible righteousness for his people.

11.
The Son arrives

Hebrews 10:5-7

In eternity past God the Father gave God the Son a people for his own with the understanding that the Son would come into this world as a man and lay down his life for them. That plan was announced to the human race after Adam and Eve sinned, and men and women began to look forward in faith to the coming of the Son of God.

The author of Hebrews brings us to that grand, sparkling moment when the Son of God rose from his throne of glory and said to the Father:

> Sacrifice and offering you did not desire,
> But a body you have prepared for me.
> In burnt offerings and sacrifices for sin
> You had no pleasure.
> Then I said, 'Behold, I have come —
> In the volume of the book it is written of me —
> To do your will, O God'
>
> (Heb. 10:5-7).

In these words, we have the Son receiving a body and revealing a spirit.

The Son receives a body

The body prepared for the Son was the body he assumed in the incarnation. The word 'incarnation' comes from a Latin word which means 'in flesh'. When we speak, therefore, about the incarnation of Christ, we are referring to his taking our humanity.

The plan of redemption to which the Father and the Son mutually agreed required the Son to take our humanity. There was no value in the blood of animals. These sacrifices had no power actually to deal with sin. The only reason God required them was as a means of pointing to the coming of the Lord Jesus Christ. The animals did not have a human nature and could not, therefore, actually take the place of human beings, and they certainly were not in a position to consent to being offered in the place of sinners. In taking the body God had prepared for him, Jesus was able to do what the animal sacrifices could never do.

The penalty for man's sin must be paid by a man. That penalty is death and the Son of God could not die apart from becoming a man. Athanasius explains, 'As the Word who is immortal and the Father's Son it was not possible for him to die, and this is the reason why he assumed a body capable of dying... He put on a body so that in the body he might find death and blot it out.'[1]

So the Second Person of the Trinity took our humanity. This is the central miracle of the Christian faith, the miracle against which all other miracles seem pale. The truly startling and staggering claim of the Christian faith is wrapped tightly and tersely in a package of four little words from the apostle Paul: 'God was in Christ' (2 Cor. 5:19).

It is possible for us to become so familiar with truth that we no longer feel the sharp, cutting edge of it. We can hear it so often that we no longer appreciate the wonder of it. But this is truly stupendous! God actually became a man. He took our flesh and our blood (Heb. 2:14). He had arms and legs, feet and hands, eyes and ears, nose and mouth.

If we had been there with the shepherds on the night the Son of God came into this world, we would have seen a real baby who cried and kicked just like any other baby. Quite often we see the baby Jesus depicted with a halo around his head, but that night in Bethlehem there was no halo. The baby in the manger was a real, human baby.

As a man the Lord Jesus experienced all that is common to men. He grew tired, hungry and thirsty. He knew what it was to feel pain and to weep tears of sorrow.

But while the Son of God took real humanity, he was no ordinary man. In taking our humanity, he did not cease to be God. Without losing or diminishing his deity, he added our humanity so that he was at one and the same time both God and man — the God-man.

The apostle John summarized it perfectly: 'And the Word became flesh and dwelt among us, and we beheld his glory, the glory as of the only begotten of the Father, full of grace and truth' (John 1:14). John saw the humanity of Christ, and there was no doubt in his mind that it was real. So he was able to speak about 'flesh'. But as he and the other disciples closely observed Jesus they saw something else — namely, beams of glory shining through the veil of his humanity so that they had to conclude that he was indeed 'the only begotten of the Father, full of grace and truth'.

Two natures; one person; and no contradiction or opposition between the two — do we understand it? Of course not. We should not expect to. This is the work of the sovereign God and, as such, it is completely above and beyond us.

The Son reveals a spirit

The Son of God did not take the body prepared for him reluctantly, or grudgingly, but gladly and willingly. There is not a trace of resistance to be found in his words. The will of the Father was his will.

Some have tried to drive a wedge between the Father and the Son on the matter of redemption. They picture God the Father as being harsh, severe and unwilling to forgive, and the Son as one who was loving and had to wring forgiveness for sinners out of his Father. Nothing could be farther from the truth. God the Father willed the salvation of sinners, and God the Son submitted to that will and perfectly carried it out.

The Son's spirit of willingness is revealed in other passages of Scripture as well. Paul says Christ did not consider equality with God as a thing to be clung to at all costs, but instead was willing to strip himself of all the trappings of deity and become a man. His spirit was such that he 'made himself of no reputation', but rather took 'the form of a servant' (Phil. 2:7). He then humbled himself even further so that he 'became obedient to ... the death of the cross' (Phil. 2:8).

The same willingness that brought the Son down from his glory was consistently expressed and reflected in his earthly life and ministry. Throughout the Gospel of John we find him saying he had come to do the Father's will (John 6:38; 7:16; 8:29; 9:4).

The Father's will finally brought Jesus to the garden of Gethsemane the night before he was crucified. Jesus knew the cross was hovering over him. He knew all about the physical and mental anguish he would have to endure. He could foresee that awful moment when he was to be completely forsaken by the Father. But still he prayed, 'Not my will, but yours, be done' (Luke 22:42).

Let us never lose sight of the fact that Jesus received a human body and revealed the spirit of humility for our sakes. The apostle Paul writes, 'For you know the grace of our Lord Jesus Christ, that though he was rich, yet for your sakes he became poor, that you through his poverty might become rich' (2 Cor. 8:9). Did you grasp what Paul is saying? Jesus did all that he did for the sake of those whom the Father had given him. It was all because of his amazing grace. There was absolutely nothing in us to commend us to him, but he willingly became one of us that he might suffer for us.

Oh, what a chasm he crossed! From heaven to earth, from heaven's glory to Bethlehem's crude stable and manger, from riches to poverty, from angels' praises to the hostility of sinners, from a perfect environment to a world of sin and shame! And it was all for us — for us!

The angels stood in awe as they beheld the Son crossing this chasm, and they were not even the beneficiaries of it. How much more should those of us who are the beneficiaries stand in awe! If they worshipped, how much more should we! We should be amazed that he would come. We should be amazed that he would come as he did. We should be amazed that he would come to do what he did.

12.
The Son affirms the cross:
at his baptism

Matthew 3:13-17

The third chapter of Matthew brings before us a remarkable sight. Here we have Jesus of Nazareth standing alongside John the Baptist in the water of the Jordan River. At first we might not see anything so remarkable in that. After all, many Jewish men were coming for John's baptism in those days. But Jesus, while he was a real man, was no ordinary man. He was nothing less than God in human flesh.

John the Baptist knew this. He had hailed Jesus as 'the Lamb of God who takes away the sin of the world' (John 1:29). That phrase was no accident, nor was it a mere flight of poetic imagination. By calling Jesus 'the Lamb of God', John was quite clearly and explicitly affirming that Jesus was the fulfilment of the promise God had given centuries before. In particular, John was linking Jesus to the Passover lamb that the children of Israel had to slay. That lamb had to be without spot or blemish.

In declaring Jesus to be the Lamb of God, John was not only saying that this was the one who had come to lay down his life as the payment for the sins of his people, but that he was also spotless and without blemish (a truth repeated by the apostle Peter in 1 Peter 1:19).

The necessity of Jesus' baptism

Now John the Baptist had a problem on his hands. Standing here beside him in the Jordan River was the sinless one, and the baptism that he, John, was practising was one of repentance. In other words, those who submitted to it were indicating that they recognized their sinful condition and were truly repenting. But Jesus had no sin and would not seem, therefore, to have any need of baptism.

John, realizing all this, said to Jesus, 'I have need to be baptized by you, and are you coming to me?' (v. 14). It is interesting to note that Jesus in no way disagreed with John. We look in vain for a single instance of Jesus ever acknowledging any personal sin. But while he accepted John's conclusion, he still insisted on being baptized. Why?

Jesus explained by simply saying, 'Permit it to be so now, for thus it is fitting for us to fulfil all righteousness' (v. 15). What was he saying? Essentially this: 'John, you must yield to me on this matter because baptism is one of the Father's righteous requirements for my mission.'

Baptism was, then, part of the plan that God the Father and God the Son had worked out before time began. That plan consisted of the Father's giving the Son a people, and the Son's agreeing to redeem them from sin by coming as their substitute and bearing the punishment due to their sin.

Jesus had no sin of his own, but he had to take the sins of his people. By standing there in those baptismal waters with John, he was publicly identifying himself with his people in their sin.

I suggest that Jesus, by taking his place there with John, was for all practical purposes saying to the Father, 'I have come to stand in the place of those people you have given me. I freely and gladly identify with them in their sin so I can serve as their substitute and pay their penalty.'

The Father's response

It therefore comes as no surprise to read that the Father responded from heaven with these words: 'This is my beloved Son, in whom I am well pleased' (v. 17). That was an expression of the Father's satisfaction with his Son's identification of himself with sinners.

We can easily fall into the trap of thinking salvation has to satisfy us. Many hear the historic Christian gospel preached and begin to pronounce judgement on various aspects of it. They hear one doctrine and say they cannot accept it. They hear another and complain that it does not seem fair. On and on they go, believing themselves to be competent arbiters of what is right about this old gospel and what is wrong. The consumer mentality has come to church these days, and the consumers feel as much at ease in choosing one doctrine and dispensing with another as they would if they were standing before a loaded buffet.

Many churches have decided the course of wisdom is not to swim against the tide, but to go with it. This was illustrated by a national advertising campaign undertaken by a denomination in the United States which featured a parishioner saying, 'Instead of trying to fit a religion, I found one to fit me.'

Against all this stands the unwavering testimony of Holy Scripture that it is God who has to be satisfied before any of us can ever hope to stand in his presence. He is the one who created us for himself. He is the sovereign Lord who has the right to require his creatures to obey his commands. He is the holy and righteous one who is insulted by the stubborn refusal of his creatures to obey his commands. And for those creatures to assume that salvation must somehow or other satisfy them is rather like asking the fox to guard the chickens, or the inmates to run the prison.

The thing that ought to amaze and astonish us is that this holy God whom we have so grievously insulted with our sins can ever be satisfied at all. The good news of the Christian message is not only that he can be satisfied, but that he actually has been satisfied through that man who stood there alongside John the Baptist in the water of the Jordan River. By identifying with sinners there and going to Calvary's cross and bearing the punishment that was due to them, Jesus has indeed satisfied the just claims of the holy, sovereign God.

The point we need to feel keenly is this: if God is satisfied with Jesus, you and I had better be satisfied with him too!

The Spirit's anointing

Another dimension of Jesus' baptism must not escape our notice. Just before the Father spoke his words of approval of his Son, the Spirit of God descended upon the Lord Jesus in the form of a dove.

The Holy Spirit, the Third Person of the Trinity, was at one with the Father and the Son in the plan of redemption. The Father gave a love-gift to the Son. The Son purchased this love-gift through his atoning death. And the Holy Spirit anointed the Son for the task and applies his atoning death to those whom the Father gave to the Son.

The emphasis at this point is on the anointing the Holy Spirit bestowed upon Jesus for the work God the Father had given him to do. That work can be divided into three parts or offices: Prophet, Priest and King.

As Prophet Jesus was to represent God to men, faithfully proclaiming his truth to them. As Priest he offered to God the perfect sacrifice for the sins of his people — himself! As King he rules over his people, provides for them and protects them.

This threefold office of the Lord Jesus Christ is an essential part of the redemptive work assigned to him by the Father. There can be no salvation for anyone apart from these three offices. The sinner is ignorant of God's truth and, therefore, needs someone to instruct him. The Lord Jesus, as Prophet, provides this. The sinner is also alienated from God and needs reconciliation. By his death on Calvary's cross, Jesus took the penalty of our sin and thereby removed the barrier between us and God. The sinner is possessed of a nature that is stubborn and rebellious and also weak and foolish in the business of living. As King, the Lord Jesus subdues and rules the sinful nature of his people as well as protecting and guiding them.

Jesus identifies with sinners, the Father approves and the Spirit anoints. Our redemption is the result of the triune God at work. It is the completed product of a united Godhead.

13.
The Son affirms the cross: in the wilderness

Matthew 4:1-11

'Baptism does not drown the devil,' was the striking response of Jerome to the teaching of Jovinian that baptism frees a person for ever from the temptations of Satan.[1] This passage makes it clear that even Jesus' baptism did not insulate him from Satan's assault.

When Jesus stood in the Jordan River with John the Baptist, he was publicly identifying himself with the people the Father had given him. That was a necessary part of the plan of redemption. It was also necessary that Jesus be tempted by Satan in the wilderness. This is made clear by each of the Gospel accounts. Matthew says, 'Jesus was led up by the Spirit into the wilderness to be tempted by the devil' (Matt. 4:1). Mark states it more forcefully: 'And immediately the Spirit drove him into the wilderness' (Mark 1:12). Luke joins Matthew in saying Jesus was 'led by the Spirit into the wilderness' (Luke 4:1).

These verses help us put the temptation of Jesus in the right perspective. If we are not careful we can picture Jesus as a poor victim of circumstances and see the plan of redemption tottering on the verge of disaster. A false reading of this passage makes Satan the challenger and has us wondering if Jesus will be able to stand up against his assault. But it was Jesus who was doing the challenging. It was part of God's plan that Jesus should encounter these temptations so that he would be fully qualified to be the Redeemer. Jesus went into the wilderness, therefore, for the express purpose of encountering Satan and defeating him. These temptations should not be viewed as tests to see if Jesus would sin, but rather as opportunities to prove that he would not. When tyre manufacturers put their tyres on a truck, hoist it high in the air and drop it, they do not do it so we can see if the tyres blow out, but to prove that they will not.

What we have in the temptations, then, is God throwing the gauntlet down. Satan had succeeded in his temptations of the first head of the human race, Adam, but another Adam was now on the scene as the representative head of redeemed humanity. The Father here sends him into the wilderness and essentially says to Satan, 'Let's see how you do with this Adam!'

In order to die for the sins of those given to him by the Father, Christ, the new Adam, had to be free from sin. Had he sinned himself, he would have had to pay the penalty for his own sin and could not, therefore, pay for the sins of anyone else.

Satan, to be sure, sought every conceivable advantage, and when he finally confronted Jesus it looked as if he had more advantages than he enjoyed in Eden. There he stalked Adam in a paradise; but here Jesus was in a wilderness. Adam had been well fed, with liberty to eat of all the trees of the garden except one; but Jesus had been fasting for forty days, and the pinch of hunger was very real. Furthermore, Adam had not been alone, having been given Eve as a companion; but the only companions the Lord Jesus had were the wild beasts (Mark 1:13).

So the stage was set. The first Adam had failed under the most favourable of circumstances, but the last Adam had now stepped into the arena to take up the fight.

Satan assailed Jesus with three temptations, each of which was designed to entice him to fail in a crucial aspect of his mission. Each of the temptations also represents a duplication of the tactics that Satan had successfully employed against Adam.

The temptation to doubt God's goodness

The first temptation was designed to entice Jesus to doubt the goodness and the care of his Father. We can call it the 'Is God really good?' temptation.

Satan began with Eve in the same way. God had allowed Adam and Eve to eat of every tree in the garden except the tree of the knowledge of good and evil. Satan attacked at that point by asking, 'Has God indeed said, "You shall not eat of every tree of the garden"?' (Gen. 3:1). His insinuation was clear. If God were really as good as he would have Adam and Eve to believe, he would have allowed them to eat of all the trees without any exceptions.

Now let us move rapidly forward in time to the scene in the wilderness. Jesus was in the wilderness after his Father had said, 'This is my beloved Son, in whom I am well pleased' (Matt. 3:17). And not only was he in the wilderness, but he was extremely hungry. So Satan moved in to suggest that if God were really his Father he would not allow him to be hungry and Jesus should, therefore, use his own power to supply for himself what the Father had failed to supply.

Had Jesus done so, he would have failed to do the very thing that he so often said he had come to do — namely, the Father's will. But Jesus did not fail. He quoted the words of Deuteronomy 8:3: 'Man shall not live by bread alone, but by every word that proceeds from the mouth of God' (Matt. 4:4). By quoting this verse, Jesus was asserting that he had no need of food in order to know the Father was good. His Word was sufficient evidence for that.

The temptation to achieve good through disobeying

The second temptation can be called the 'Bad is good' temptation — that is, that something that appears to be evil is not really evil at all.

In the Garden of Eden, Satan assured Eve that the good she and Adam stood to receive — becoming like God — far outweighed any evil they might incur (Gen. 3:4-5). It worked so well in Eden that Satan tried the same approach here. This temptation took up the issue Jesus had raised in responding to the first temptation. Jesus had asserted that the Word of God was sufficient to prove the goodness of God, so Satan essentially said, 'I see you trust the Word of God. That's good. Why not prove the truth of it by leaping from the pinnacle of the temple? After all, the Word of God says he will send his angels to make sure no harm comes to you.'

So Satan was asserting that Jesus would not die, but rather would achieve great good. Not only would the Father ensure his safety, but his Messiahship would be proven beyond any shadow of doubt. Hence good would spring from what appeared to be evil.

Jesus firmly responded to this temptation by again quoting from the book of Deuteronomy: 'It is written again, "You shall not tempt the Lord your God"' (Matt. 4:7). To seek to force the Father to do what we want done when we want it done is not to trust, but to doubt. Had Jesus failed to trust the Father with whom he had planned the redemption of sinners, there would have been no redemption.

The temptation to act on the basis of emotion

The final temptation can be called the 'Doesn't this look good?' temptation. Satan succeeded with Eve by enticing her to look upon the beauty of the forbidden tree and to note how pleasant its fruit appeared to be (Gen. 3:6). In doing so, he short-circuited the way in which God designed Adam and Eve to function. That way consisted of truth coming to the mind, the emotions being moved by that truth and then the mind and emotions together moving the will. But Satan succeeded in bypassing the mind with Eve so that she chose on the basis of emotion rather than the truth of God.

Satan attempted the same with Jesus by giving him a panoramic view of all the kingdoms of the world. The emphasis was on the splendour, the beauty, the desirability of these kingdoms — that is, how they appealed to the eye. Satan was clearly seeking to excite the affections of Jesus and entice him to put them above everything else. He was seeking to get Jesus to disobey what he knew to be the truth of God. God's will was for Jesus to have dominion through his death on the cross. But Satan tried to destroy Jesus' commitment to that truth by offering him dominion without his having to travel the pathway of the cross.

Jesus responded by drawing from Deuteronomy 6:13: 'You shall worship the Lord your God, and him only you shall serve' (Matt. 4:10). Given the opportunity to renounce the Father who sent him and the cross to which he was sent, the Lord Jesus Christ powerfully affirmed both. He was victorious over Satan.

But let us never forget what that victory was all about. It was not merely for himself that Jesus fought. He came to purchase those whom the Father had given him, and this victory allowed him to die in their stead. He could not have died for others if he had any sin of his own. His victory is our victory because it demonstrated him to be the spotless Lamb of God and qualified to die for us.

14.
The Son affirms the cross:
in his public ministry

A strange teaching has made the rounds for several years that Jesus did not come to this earth to die on the cross — that he came rather to set up an earthly kingdom, but he was taken by surprise when the Jews to whom he offered his kingdom rejected him. According to this view, the Lord Jesus went to the cross and died as something of an afterthought.

Scripture, however, makes it clear that Jesus had the cross clearly in view from the very beginning of his public ministry, and he kept it in view throughout the course of that ministry. This can readily be seen in the pictures Jesus uses to describe his mission and in his discourses.

The pictures Jesus uses

The Gospel accounts of the years of his public ministry relate several instances in which Jesus used very graphic and descriptive terms to describe his impending death on the cross. These images make it obvious that the cross was never far from his mind. He saw his public ministry as a prelude and the means of approach to it.

An appointment to be kept

After returning from the wilderness where he was tempted, and immediately before launching his public ministry, the Lord Jesus and his disciples attended a wedding feast at Cana. Suddenly his mother approached him with the word that the host had run out of wine. This was highly embarrassing! She clearly expected Jesus to take some kind of action.

Jesus responded to Mary by saying, 'Woman, what does your concern have to do with me? My hour has not yet come' (John 2:4). Jesus was not being rude to his mother. He was merely pointing out that his concern was different from hers. She had a temporal concern — the wine — but he, while not indifferent to that need, had a far more pressing concern which he expressed in terms of an 'hour'.

Jesus' mention of this 'hour', or 'time', was only the first of several in John's Gospel (John 7:6,8,30; 8:20; 12:23; 13:1; 17:1). Each time we find it we may say that, in the words of William Hendriksen, it clearly indicates 'Christ's conscious-ness of the fact that he was accomplishing a task entrusted to him by the Father, every detail of which had been definitely marked off in the eternal decree, so that for each act there was a stipulated moment'.[1]

An assignment to be completed

Jesus' death on the cross was assigned to him by God the Father in eternity past. Jesus came to this world knowing that was his assignment, and when he spoke of his coming death he often referred to it in those terms.

One of the words he most frequently used in connection with his mission was 'sent'. This was something he was assigned to do. One of the phrases he most frequently used is 'the Father's will'. Jesus came to do what the Father willed him to do. He had been assigned the work by another and sent to perform it.

The Gospel of John records several instances where Jesus used the expressions 'sent' and 'the Father's will' together. In John 4:34 he says, 'My food is to do the will of him who sent me, and to finish his work.' In John 5:30 he remarks, 'I do not seek my own will but the will of the Father who sent me.' In John 6:38-40 Jesus explains his mission in these terms: 'For I have come down from heaven, not to do my own will, but the will of him who sent me. This is the will of the Father who sent me, that of all he has given me I should lose nothing, but should raise it up at the last day. And this is the will of him who sent me, that everyone who sees the Son and believes in him may have everlasting life; and I will raise him up at the last day.'

Jesus also spoke of the cross in another way that conveys the idea of an assignment. It was a command to be kept. In John 10:17-18 Jesus says, 'Therefore my Father loves me, because I lay down my life that I may take it again. No one takes it from me, but I lay it down of myself. I have power to lay it down, and I have power to take it again. This command I have received from my Father.'

An anguish to be endured

Jesus knew that the cross would mean depths of anguish and agony that no one had ever experienced before. Luke records him as saying, 'I came to send fire on the earth, and how I wish it were already kindled! But I have a baptism to be baptized with, and how distressed I am till it is accomplished!' (Luke 12:49-50).

What dramatic emblems Jesus chose to represent his death — fire and baptism! Fire is linked in Scripture with judgement.

His people deserve the fire of God's judgement because of their sins, but it was going to consume Jesus instead. The Passover lamb was to be completely roasted in fire, and Jesus, the Lamb of God, was to be roasted in the fire of God's judgement on Calvary's cross. The suffering and anguish were to be fierce. No wonder Jesus expressed his wish that the fire were already kindled!

Baptism is the complete submerging of the body in water. It carries the idea of being overcome or overwhelmed. As Jesus looked forward to the cross, he was under no illusions about what it meant for him. The words of the psalmist would be all too fitting for that occasion: 'All your waves and billows have gone over me' (Ps. 42:7).

The anguish of the cross is also conveyed by Jesus' use of the figure of the cup. In Gethsemane, a scene which we shall consider more fully in a later chapter, Jesus prayed for the cup to pass from him (Matt. 26:39; Mark 14:36; Luke 22:42). He came from that time of prayer saying, 'Shall I not drink the cup which my Father has given me?' (John 18:11).

That cup was filled with the bitterness of the wrath of God. It had to be drained to the very dregs if there was to be redemption for the people of God. We cannot begin to imagine the anguish it entailed for the Lord Jesus Christ to put the cup of God's wrath to his lips when up to this point he had enjoyed nothing but unbroken communion with the Father. Nothing could have been more painful to the Saviour. Let us never forget that he pressed that cup of wrath to his lips and drank it dry so his people might drink from the cup of salvation!

A ransom to be paid

Jesus further spoke of the cross as the place where a ransom was to be paid. It was immediately after the mother of James and John asked the Lord if her sons could be granted the privilege of sitting one at his right and the other at his left in the final disposition of his kingdom. The other ten disciples were enraged at this suggestion, and Jesus seized the moment to instruct them about servanthood: 'And whoever desires to be first among you, let him be your slave — just as the Son of man did not come to be served, but to serve, and to give his life a ransom for many' (Matt. 20:27-28).

That word 'ransom' brings us to the nature of Jesus' death on the cross. This word, used on only two occasions in the New Testament (Mark 10:45 is the other), takes us into the realm of slavery. It refers to paying the price that was necessary to set a slave free.

The sober affirmation of the Scriptures is that each and every one of us is by nature a slave. Sin has not only enslaved us; it has also brought us under the wrath of God. But the good news is that we can be redeemed from our slavery. To effect that redemption Jesus died on the cross. There he paid the price of redemption. He gave up his own life in exchange for the lives of 'many' slaves to sin. Who are these 'many?' Those very ones whom the Father had given him before time began.

A type to be fulfilled

We also find Jesus proclaiming the cross the night Nicodemus came to him. This ruler of the Jews came with the assumption that the Messiah's kingdom would be of this earth and that he would automatically be included by virtue of his birth. The Lord Jesus had some shattering words for him. His kingdom was spiritual in nature and one could only enter it through a spiritual birth. And this spiritual birth could only be made available through the death of the Messiah. So Jesus drew his conversation with Nicodemus to a close by proclaiming the cross in these words: 'And as Moses lifted up the serpent in the wilderness, even so must the Son of Man be lifted up' (John 3:14).

Jesus was taking Nicodemus back to that time in the nation's history when God sent poisonous serpents into the camp of Israel to punish the people for the grievous sin of speaking against the Lord and against Moses. Bites from those serpents caused many to die, but the Lord also graciously provided a means of deliverance. He commanded Moses to make a serpent of brass and put it on a pole in the camp. All who looked upon that pole were cured of the deadly snake bite (Num. 21:4-9).

Jesus saw that brass serpent on the pole as an apt picture of his own death on the cross. It was a type, or figure, of his being lifted up on the cross.

The following parallels between that serpent of brass and Christ are suggested by Henry Mahan:

1. The serpent was made in the likeness of the fiery serpents, and Christ was made in the likeness of sinful flesh (Rom. 8:3; Phil. 2:7).

2. The serpent of brass had no venom, and Christ had no sin.

3. The brazen serpent was lifted up on a pole, and Christ was lifted up on the cross.

4. The serpent on the pole was the only remedy for the snake bite, and Christ on the cross is the only remedy for sin.

5. To receive healing from the poisonous bites, the people only had to look at the brass serpent, and to receive healing from sin, we must look to Jesus' atoning death on the cross.[2]

The discourses of Jesus

John includes in his Gospel several discourses not found in the other Gospels, including the one on the bread of life (John 6:32-58) and the one on the good shepherd (John 10:1-18).

The bread of life discourse (John 6:32-58)

This discourse is of particular interest. When Jesus began it he was the darling of the multitudes. By the time it ended he was down to twelve disciples, one of whom was false.

How had Jesus become so popular? The day before he had miraculously fed five thousand people in the wilderness, an act which fanned the people into a fever pitch of excitement to make him king (John 6:15).

Jesus had short-circuited their plans on that day by authoritatively dismissing the multitude and by making his way (miraculously, we learn from John 6:16-25) to Capernaum. But many were not willing to leave matters there. They followed him to Capernaum. Their obsession with their next meal opened the door for Jesus to address their far deeper need for spiritual bread that alone can satisfy. That all sounds innocent enough. How did Jesus, in the course of one discourse, manage to alienate all but a handful of his audience?

He covered those topics that the natural man finds most offensive and disconcerting. The doctrine of *man's inability* is here. The Lord Jesus says, 'No one can come to me unless the Father who sent me draws him' (John 6:44). The doctrine of *the supreme authority of the Lord Jesus Christ* is here. He is the one who came down from heaven (John 6:33,38,41, 42,50,51,58), and he is the only one who has authority to grant everlasting life and to raise from the dead (John 6:40). The doctrine of *blood atonement* is also here. Jesus is spiritual bread for us by virtue of his death. He says, 'The bread that I shall give is my flesh, which I shall give for the life of the world' (John 6:51). And that blood atonement must be appropriated. His flesh must be eaten, and his blood must be drunk (John 6:53-55). What is it to eat the flesh of Christ and drink his blood? It is to believe in him as the only Lord and Saviour (John 6:40,47).

All of this was too much to bear for the vast majority of Jesus' hearers — even as it is too much for many today to bear — and they walked away. And Jesus let them go. He refused to remove the cross from his agenda even though it caused many to stumble.

The good shepherd discourse

The Lord Jesus continued to adhere to that cross when he addressed the religious leaders of Jerusalem. The fact that they were false shepherds was amply confirmed by their callous treatment of the blind man whom Jesus had healed. Because he freely admitted that Jesus had opened his eyes, these leaders cast him out of the synagogue (John 9:34).

Their action prompted Jesus to draw a sharp distinction between false shepherds and true shepherds (John 10:1-10). The true shepherds lead their sheep through the door into the sheepfold. The door is Jesus, and a true minister always points to him as the only way to become part of the people of God. The problem with false ministers is that they have no door for people to go through.

Jesus followed that up by drawing a further distinction — between himself as the Good Shepherd and the religious leaders as mere hirelings (John 10:11-18).

In drawing this distinction, the Lord Jesus again repeatedly stressed his soon-coming death. He says, 'Therefore my Father loves me, because I lay down my life that I may take it again. No one takes it from me, but I lay it down of myself. I have power to lay it down, and I have power to take it again. This command I have received from my Father' (John 10:17-18). His death was the essential ingredient in his shepherding of his sheep. Through that death he was to purchase them as his sheep.

The images the Lord Jesus used and the discourses he presented make it abundantly clear that his impending death on the cross was much on his mind and on his lips. It could not possibly be any other way. He came to this earth for the express purpose of dying on that cross. It could hardly be considered the focal point of his life if he never spoke of it. But, as we have noted, he did speak of it — early and often, and in speaking of it he made it obvious that heaven's plan was his priority. His fidelity to that plan should fill the hearts of believers with immense gratitude. Christ's faithfulness in fulfilling his mission opened heaven's door.

15.
The Son affirms the cross: with his disciples

Matt. 16:13-23

A wide disparity exists between the public and private sides of some individuals. They say one thing in public and another in private. It was not so with Jesus. The private Jesus was the same as the public Jesus. The private Jesus is the one we find in the Gospel accounts of his dealings with his disciples. The same Jesus who spoke forcefully about his death in public did the same in private with his disciples.

Some of Jesus' words to his disciples about his death were not entirely private. While they were directed primarily to the disciples, bystanders also took them in. It was often the case when Jesus taught his disciples that several others 'listened in'. Jesus' poignant description of his death as being consumed with a fire and undergoing a baptism (Luke 12:50) falls into this category. After he spoke these words, Luke tells us he turned to 'the multitudes' (Luke 12:54), who had evidently been there all along. There are, however, three distinct instances in which Jesus spoke only to his disciples.

The three predictions

These three predictions are quite distinctly marked out and catalogued by Matthew, Mark and Luke. The first of them came at Caesarea Philippi (Matt. 16:21; Mark 8:31-33; Luke 9:21-22). The second was in Galilee (Matt. 17:22-23; Mark 9:30-32; Luke 9:43-45). The third came on the Lord's final journey to Jerusalem (Matt. 20:17-19; Mark 10:32-34; Luke 18:31-34).

Certain things leap out at us from these predictions. One is the emphasis Jesus placed on the necessity of his death. It was not that this might happen to him if he did not handle the religious leaders the right way. No, it was much more than that. There was a 'must' to it. His death on the cross was ordained before the world began. For that end he came to this world.

We must also be struck by the precise detail the Lord Jesus included in these predictions. He spoke of being betrayed, mocked and scourged. And, although the religious leaders had attempted at various times to put him to death by stoning, the Lord Jesus specifically said he would be crucified (Matt. 20:19).

In these predictions the Lord also emphasized that crucifixion was not to be the final word for him. He would also be raised from the dead.

The varying responses of the disciples

The disciples responded to these predictions in a variety of ways. Mark and Luke tell us they did not understand one of the predictions and were afraid to ask him (Mark 9:32; Luke 9:45). On another occasion, Luke simply says the 'saying was hidden from them' (Luke 18:34). Matthew says they were 'exceedingly sorrowful' when Jesus predicted his death for the second time (Matt. 17:23).

The best-known of Jesus' predictions to his disciples — with the best-known of the responses — is the one that Jesus made at Caesarea Philippi. While Jesus had made allusions to the cross in his public ministry, they remained vague and shadowy as far as the disciples were concerned. These were allusions that perhaps temporarily brought a furrow to their brows, but in those heady, intoxicating days of Jesus' early ministry such references were quickly dismissed. However, there came a day when the disciples could no longer dismiss Jesus' talk about that mysterious hour and about the ransom he would provide. At Caesarea Philippi Jesus thrust the cross upon them in unmistakable terms.

It all began innocently enough. Jesus asked them, 'Who do men say that I, the Son of Man, am?' (Matt. 16:13). There was no shortage of answers, and the disciples rattled them off: John the Baptist, Elijah, Jeremiah, one of the prophets.

But then Jesus made the question more pointed: 'But who do you say that I am?' (v. 15). Simon Peter was ready with the answer: 'You are the Christ, the Son of the living God' (v. 16).

None of the disciples was prepared for where all this was intended to lead: 'From that time Jesus began to show to his disciples that he must go to Jerusalem, and suffer many things from the elders and chief priests and scribes, and be killed, and be raised again the third day' (v. 21).

Evidently Simon Peter failed to hear the 'must' in that statement. Taking Jesus by the arm, he steered him to one side and lectured him: 'Far be it from you, Lord; this shall not happen to you!' (v. 22).

On occasions Jesus had some very strong and stinging words for the hypocritical religious leaders who were leading many astray. We find him, for instance, referring to them as 'whitewashed tombs', 'serpents' and a 'brood of vipers' (Matt. 23:27,33). But he never spoke sterner words to one of his disciples than these: 'Get behind me, Satan! You are an offence to me, for you are not mindful of the things of God, but the things of men' (v. 23). Why did Jesus answer Peter in such stern words? Why did he go so far as actually to call his disciple 'Satan'? Was he not guilty of exaggeration here?

This was no mere squabble over some fine point of obscure doctrine. In taking Jesus aside to rebuke him, Simon Peter was guilty of attacking the very purpose for which Jesus had come. Had it not been for that cross looming in his future, the Son of God would not even have been standing in the presence of Simon. That cross, and that cross alone, had brought the Son of God to earth from heaven's glory. That cross defined his mission.

J. Glyn Owen rightly says, 'Peter is trying to protect the very one whom he has recently acknowledged to be divine from what seems to him the folly of his divinity. Peter is trying to divert Jesus from the overmastering "must" which he has just disclosed as being indispensable to the fulfilment of his mission.'[1]

But Jesus meant that 'must'! He was not registering his viewpoint on what was likely to happen in the light of current trends, as political analysts do today. That cross had to happen! God's sovereign decree demanded it. Man's sin demanded it. The promises of the Old Testament demanded it. The heart of Jesus himself demanded it.

By suggesting the cross was not necessary, Simon Peter had moved from the stance he had just taken — the humble disciple confessing the truth about Jesus — to a new position altogether. He had moved from the disciple's shoes to occupy Satan's shoes. In the wilderness Satan attempted to get Jesus to bypass the cross, and Simon Peter was now doing the same. When a man acts like Satan he deserves to go by that name!

In addition to pointing out Simon's new stance, the Lord Jesus also called him back to his former one. 'Get behind me!' was a scorching reminder that the place for Christ's disciples is always following along behind their Lord and never leading him.

There is much here for us to take home to heart. Jesus' predictions of his death constitute yet another of his affirmations of the cross, and that gives us cause to rejoice. We must not, however, leave it at that. Our Lord's rebuke of Simon Peter gives us insight into the Lord's attitude to all attempts to remove or diminish the cross.

Many churches and pastors appear to be repeating Simon Peter's error. Thinking they know more than the one they call 'Lord', they downplay the holiness of God, the guilt of sinners and the cross as the way for God and sinners to be reconciled. How the church today needs the sober reminder that our Lord regards all attempts to diminish that cross as nothing less than siding with Satan! We hear much these days about the need for the church to go forward. Meanwhile her Lord calls her to go backward until she is behind him again. And being behind him will always mean cherishing and proclaiming his cross.

16.
The Son affirms the cross:
the transfiguration

Matthew 17:1-8; Mark 9:2-8; Luke 9:28-36

Our word 'transfiguration' comes from the Greek word *'metamorphoomai'*, from which we get the word 'metamorphosis'. When something 'metamorphoses' it undergoes a striking change in appearance or character.

The transfiguration and the person of Christ

Scripture tells us the Lord Jesus Christ was transfigured before three of his disciples. R. C. Sproul gets at the essence of what happened with these words: 'The prefix trans- means literally "across". In the transfiguration a limit or barrier is crossed. We might call it a crossing of the line between the natural and the supernatural, between the human and the divine. It crosses a boundary of dimensions into the realm of God.'[1]

In the presence of Peter, James and John, the Lord Jesus crossed that barrier between the human and the divine. He was substantially changed. While he was still very much a part of earth, he took on a heavenly appearance.

Charles Eerdman sums it up in this way: 'It is as if the monarch had been walking in disguise; only occasionally beneath his humble garment has been revealed a glimpse of the purple and the gold. Here, for an hour, the disguise is withdrawn and the King appears in his real majesty and in the regal splendour of his divine glory.'[2]

When the Second Person of the Trinity took our humanity, he did not cease to be God. The deity was still there, but it was veiled. In the transfiguration, the veil was, as it were, drawn back so that the deity that was always there could be clearly seen.

It was an amazing sight. Matthew says Jesus' face 'shone like the sun, and his clothes became as white as the light' (Matt. 17:2). Mark says, 'His clothes became shining, exceedingly white, like snow, such as no launderer on earth can whiten them' (Mark 9:3). Luke adds this word: 'The appearance of his face was altered, and his robe became white and glistening' (Luke 9:29). R. C. Sproul sums it up in this terse comment: 'The glory of Christ perhaps never became more evident than at his transfiguration.'[3]

The sight of the transfigured Christ was astounding enough in and of itself, but the Scriptures include another astounding thing. They tell us Moses and Elijah also appeared as glorified beings and talked with him.

Why Moses and Elijah? Kent Hughes answers, 'Both these men had previously conversed with God on mountaintops — Moses on Mt Sinai (Exodus 31:18) and Elijah on Mt Horeb (1 Kings 19:9ff.). These both had been shown God's glory. Both also had famous departures from this earth. Moses died on Mt Nebo, and God had buried him in a grave known only to himself. Elijah was taken up in a chariot of fire. Moses was the great lawgiver, and Elijah was the great prophet. Moses was the *founder* of Israel's religious economy, and Elijah was the *restorer* of it. Together they were an ultimate summary of the Old Testament economy'[4] (italics are his).

Christ transfigured and appearing with the glorified Moses and Elijah — what was it all about?

The transfiguration and the work of Christ

Scripture does not leave us to our own speculations. It should not escape our attention that each of the three Gospel accounts contains a distinct reference to the timing of it. Matthew and Mark are very precise: it was six days after Jesus had predicted — and Peter contradicted — his death (Matt. 17:1; Mark 9:2). Luke, on the other hand, is content to approximate the time: 'about eight days' (Luke 9:28).

The fact that each of the Gospel writers relates the transfiguration to what had taken place at Caesarea Philippi indicates that we are to interpret it in the light of what transpired there. And the fact that the discussion at Caesarea Philippi centred on Jesus' death on the cross means the transfiguration must be related to that cross. Luke makes this connection clear by saying the transfigured Christ discussed with Moses and Elijah 'his decease which he was about to accomplish at Jerusalem' (Luke 9:31).

It is striking that Jesus' death is spoken of as something that he was going to 'accomplish' rather than suffer. Jesus was not just a passive victim when he died there on Calvary's cross. He was actively pursuing the plan that he and the Father had agreed upon. He knew in advance that this was going to happen. He went up that mountain with the awareness that he was going to be transfigured and that he would meet Moses and Elijah. By going there he was again affirming the cross upon which he and the Father had agreed in eternity past.

The whole episode came to a conclusion with the Father again speaking from heaven: 'This is my beloved Son. Hear him!' (Luke 9:35). By his presence there on the mount, the Son was affirming the cross, and by speaking from heaven, the Father was affirming his Son. Father and Son were still together on the matter of the cross.

But the words of the Father must also be related to Caesarea Philippi. There the Lord Jesus clearly predicted for his disciples in a very explicit manner that his Messiahship meant execution at the hands of the religious leaders. And there Peter, after confessing in a sterling manner the deity of the Lord Jesus, took it upon himself to contradict his Lord.

We can imagine Simon Peter going over and over in his mind the scene at Caesarea Philippi during the days that followed. Had he been right to proclaim Jesus as the Son of God? How could the Son of God die at the hands of wicked men? How could such a Messiah possibly fulfil the Old Testament prophecies?

Six days after the events which plunged him into mental turmoil, Peter had his answer. The fact that Jesus took on a heavenly appearance proved indisputably that he was the Son of God from heaven. And his appearing there with Moses and Elijah to talk specifically about his death indicated that a dying Messiah was exactly what the Law and the Prophets had foretold.

At Caesarea Philippi Simon Peter gives evidence of eroded faith. He had by this time been associated with Jesus for so long and on such an intimate basis that he no longer felt the sense of awe and wonder he once did. Prolonged association with Christ had eroded the awe he had felt back in the days when the Lord first called him to be a disciple (Luke 5:8). There was, therefore, a readiness on his part to lecture Jesus and to dispute with him.

There was to be yet another faltering step for Peter. While he was basking in the glow of transfigured glory, he blurted out, 'Master, it is good for us to be here; and let us make three tabernacles: one for you, one for Moses, and one for Elijah' (Luke 9:33). That was definitely a faltering step. It not only placed the Lord Jesus on the same level as Moses and Elijah, but it also sought to perpetuate the experience. And that, of course, meant stopping short of the cross.

Such was Peter's ill-considered response to the transfiguration, but it is safe to say the transfiguration forcefully brought the awe of Christ back to Simon Peter. There he and the others were made to realize afresh that Jesus was not just a mere man who could be mistaken and needed to be corrected, but was God in flesh. And, therefore, what he had to say about his approaching death must be accepted.

Glyn Owen says the transfiguration changed Peter's mind about the cross. 'He learned that God knows better. He learned that Moses and Elijah know better. He learned that heaven knows better than earth.'[5] Then Owen adds this word of application: 'Blessed is the man who can change his mind like that, in accordance with heavenly understanding.'[6]

17.
The Son affirms the cross: the triumphal entry

John 12:12-19

At first glance Jesus' triumphant entry into Jerusalem may seem to be anything but an affirmation of the cross. The crowds were certainly not affirming the death of Jesus on the cross — quite the contrary! Caught in a feverish excitement, they wanted Jesus to claim his throne. Jesus had evidently succeeded. What need was there now for the cross?

While the cross was the farthest thing from the minds of the enthusiastic throng, in the mind of Jesus it remained where it had always been — at the forefront of his thinking. The triumphal entry did not take him by surprise. It was not a cause for him to reconsider. Indeed, it was an integral part of his journey to the cross. It was not a detour down a side-street, but part of his direct route to the cross.

To understand and appreciate this we must first realize that this triumphal entry did not just 'happen' to Jesus. He was not just the passive recipient of it. He was in charge of it. He is here the conductor who blends the many instruments of his orchestra into the symphony he wants to hear. What had Jesus done to create this event?

Well, first there was that journey to Jerusalem. There was none like it. It began with the disciples noticing something of a change in his demeanour. Luke mentions this. He puts it in these words: 'Now it came to pass, when the time had come for him to be received up, that he steadfastly set his face to go to Jerusalem' (Luke 9:51). This steadfast determination was a fulfilment of Isaiah's prophecy: 'Therefore I have set my face like a flint, and I know that I will not be ashamed' (Isa. 50:7).

This journey to Jerusalem was different from those that had preceded it. It was Jesus' last journey there. It was not, as was the case with the other pilgrims, for the purpose of observing the Passover, but rather for the purpose of becoming the Passover Lamb by being sacrificed on the cross. This journey to Jerusalem had been carefully marked on heaven's calendar before the world began and when the time finally arrived Jesus, always resolute, became even more focused and intense.

This, of course, could not have been detected by the multitudes. But Jesus' journey to Jerusalem was to feature some things they could not possibly miss. There were those ten lepers that he healed as 'He passed through the midst of Samaria and Galilee' (Luke 17:11). Then there was the healing of blind Bartimaeus and his companion as Jesus made his way out of Jericho (Matt. 20:29-34; Mark 10:46-52; Luke 18:35-43). To crown it all, there was that grand moment when, just outside Jerusalem at Bethany, Jesus stood before the tomb of the dead Lazarus and cried, 'Lazarus, come forth!' (John 11:43). And Lazarus, 'bound hand and foot with grave-clothes,' came out of the grave (John 11:44).

Thousands of pilgrims were themselves on the road to Jerusalem for the Passover as Jesus did these things. Many saw these wonders. And those who did not see them soon heard about them. Word spread like wildfire. And the more the pilgrims heard, the more excited they became. Surely, the Messiah was among them! All that remained was for him to claim his throne.

For his part Jesus retired from the public eye to Ephraim (John 11:54) and then, six days before the Passover, returned to Bethany to spend some time with his friends, Mary, Martha and Lazarus (John 12:1). His presence there quickly became known and many made their way from Jerusalem to see both Jesus and Lazarus (John 12:9).

The point we must not miss is that Jesus was not surprised by all this excitement. He created it by his acts of healing and by raising Lazarus from the dead. That euphoria and excitement had to be in place for him to keep his appointment with the cross.

Sunday morning arrived and Jesus, who had generated all this excitement, now took full advantage of it. He continued to be the orchestrator.

In regal fashion, he issued crisp commands to his disciples: 'Go and find a colt... Loose it... Bring it...' If anyone were to ask what they were doing, they were to respond: 'Because the Lord has need of him' (Luke 19:31). This, by the way, is the only time in the Gospels in which Jesus refers to himself as Lord.

The colt, on which no one had ever ridden, seems to have recognized its Creator and to have offered no resistance, and Jesus began to make his way to the city of Jerusalem. Having taken notice of these preparations, some assumed Jesus was about to 'make his move'. They ran to the city of Jerusalem to spread the news. A large throng made their way from the city towards Bethany. Meanwhile another large crowd accompanied him from Bethany. Somewhere between Bethany and Jerusalem the two throngs merged. A glorious, intoxicating euphoria reigned, as the people waved the branches they had chopped off the palm trees lining the road and shouted 'Hosanna' ('Save now!'). Jerusalem had never seen anything to match it.

We should note that Jesus willingly accepted the acclamation of this multitude. On previous occasions he had instructed people not to say that he was the Messiah. But here he offered no objection to the surging throng crying, 'Blessed is the King who comes in the name of the Lord! Peace in heaven and glory in the highest!' (Luke 19:38). And when the Pharisees demanded that he rebuke the people, Jesus simply responded: 'I tell you that if these should keep silent, the stones would immediately cry out' (Luke 19:40).

What is going on in this scene? What does all this have to do with the cross of Christ? How can this be considered as a further affirmation of the cross by Jesus? The apostle John gives us the answer: 'The Pharisees therefore said among themselves, "You see that you are accomplishing nothing. Look, the world has gone after him!"' (John 12:19). This is a statement of sheer terror on the part of the Pharisees. Yes, they wanted to kill Jesus (John 11:53), but it is a certainty that they did not want to do it during the Passover while Jerusalem was crowded with pilgrims. After the Passover, when things were back to normal, when it could be done quietly — that was the time to kill Jesus.

But the Pharisees' timetable was not God's. His Son must not only die on the cross; he must also die at exactly the right time. He had to die during the Passover as the Lamb of God represented by the original Passover under Moses. By creating the tremendous atmosphere of excitement and by carefully orchestrating his entrance into Jerusalem, the Lord Jesus Christ was doing nothing less than forcing the religious leaders to accept his and the Father's timetable. So, far from the triumphal entry's being at odds with Jesus' plan to go to the cross, it was a ringing affirmation of his intention to go there at precisely the time the Father had ordained.

18.
The Son affirms the cross:
the upper room

John 13-17

We have seen the Lord Jesus affirming the cross at various junctures in his life and ministry. He never swerved from it or sought a detour around it. That cross was necessary to purchase the redemption of those given him by the Father, and such was his heart of love for the Father and for those given him by the Father that he wholeheartedly endorsed and embraced that cross.

Chapters 13-17 of John's Gospel bring before us the consoling truth that the Son of God faithfully affirmed that cross until the very end. There is a sacredness and an awesomeness that hovers over these chapters. It is now the night before the crucifixion. From the very beginning of his ministry, Jesus had spoken about the cross in terms of an appointed 'hour' (John 2:4). That 'hour' was never far from his thoughts (7:6; 12:23).

As we join Jesus and his disciples in the upper room, that appointed time is only hours away. The dark storm clouds of the cross have gathered around Jesus and are about to break with fury upon his head. But even the close proximity of the cross is not enough to make Jesus swerve from it. That resolute, unrelenting approach continues here. The darkness deepens, but the Saviour marches straight ahead.

John's powerful, measured opening says it all: 'Now before the feast of the Passover, when Jesus knew that his hour had come that he should depart from this world to the Father, having loved his own who were in the world, he loved them to the end' (John 13:1). 'To the end' — thank God, Jesus didn't stop short of the cross!

How did Jesus affirm the cross during those hours with his disciples in the upper room?

A vivid picture of Jesus' redeeming work

First, he vividly portrayed the essential meaning of it (John 13:3-5,12).

The details of what Jesus did that night were clearly and indelibly etched on John's mind. As he looked back on it, he was able to recall seven distinct stages.

1. Jesus rose from supper (v. 4).
2. He laid aside his garments (v. 4).
3. He girded himself with a towel (v. 4).
4. He poured water into a basin (v. 5).
5. He washed the feet of the disciples (v. 5).
6. He put his garments on again (v. 12).
7. He sat down (v. 12).

Is this not a very precise picture of what Jesus did to provide redemption? He rose from his throne, laid aside his glory, girded himself as a servant, poured out his life's blood, cleansed us from the defilement of sin by that pouring out, took up his glory again and sat down at the right hand of God. The disciples did not understand this picture until later, but Jesus understood what he was doing, and by doing it affirmed once more his glad acceptance of the cross.

A challenge to the adversary

Secondly, he openly challenged Satan (John 14:30-31).

With the words he spoke in these verses, the Lord indicated that he would not have a great deal more to say to his disciples. His explanation for this, in the words of John Brown, was that he was 'to be otherwise and fully engaged'.[1]

What was about to engage the Lord? He answers in these words: 'The ruler of this world is coming.' So the Lord was about to enter into dreadful combat with Satan himself.

The Lord Jesus had now arrived at the night before he was to fulfil the Father's command and provide redemption for sinners. And Satan, recognizing the importance of this occasion, was about to muster all the forces of hell and launch, as it were, one final, all-out assault against the Lord Jesus Christ. You and I will never understand this side of eternity all that was involved in that dreadful combat, but we may be sure that Satan's design was to thwart the plan of redemption. Perhaps his strategy was to persuade Jesus at the last moment to sidestep the assignment the Father had given him in eternity past.

Whatever his strategy, we know from our Lord's own words that Satan was coming to meet him in these hours before the cross, and we know that the Lord Jesus was ready for his assault. Before he went out to meet Satan, he assured his disciples that Satan 'has nothing' in him.

What was the Lord saying? There was absolutely nothing Satan could find in him to jeopardize in any way the work of redemption he was about to perform. There was no unwillingness for Satan to seize and use in any way. There was no disposition to avoid the cross. There was no thought of backing away. We may picture it in this way. Satan had, as it were, struck a match and stood with it burning in his hand, but there was no dry tinder or kindling in Jesus to which the match could be set.

If there was nothing in Jesus for Satan to use, what, we may well ask, was there in Jesus? For one thing, there was an eager willingness on his part to 'get on with it'. He was ready to encounter Satan and proceed with the work of redemption. He said to his disciples, '[Satan] is coming... Arise, let us go from here' (vv. 30-31). Another thing to be found in Jesus that night was profound love for the Father. The reason Jesus gave for refusing to swerve from the cross was 'that the world may know that I love the Father, and as the Father gave me commandment, so I do' (v. 31).

A prayer of affirmation

The third way in which Jesus affirmed the cross during these hours in the upper room was through prayer to the Father (17:1-26).

Some think this prayer either had to be offered on the way to the garden of Gethsemane or as part of Jesus' praying there. They take Jesus' words, 'Arise, let us go from here' (14:31), to mean Jesus and his disciples immediately made their way out of the upper room.

The contents of the prayer suggest, however, that Jesus intended all his disciples to hear it, and that there must, therefore, have been a lapse of several minutes between Jesus' announcement of their departure and the departure itself. Or it could very well be that Jesus paused along the way to the garden and offered this prayer. Whatever the precise setting of this prayer, it is another clear affirmation from Jesus that he gladly accepted the work of the cross.

The prayer itself falls into three parts. First, Jesus prayed for himself (vv. 1-5), then for those disciples who were there with him (vv. 6-19) and finally for all those who would become his disciples in the future (vv. 20-26).

Embedded in this prayer are certain distinct evidences that the Son heartily endorsed the cross and wholly submitted to it.

First, there is *Jesus' repeated reference to God as 'Father'* (a total of six times in this prayer and, by the way, over a hundred times in John's Gospel). This is enough in and of itself to convince us that Jesus approached the cross without sullenness or resentment. He was going there because the Father whom he loved had placed that cross before him, and he saw that cross as the means by which he could glorify the Father (vv. 1,4-5).

Then there is *his repeated use of the word 'given'* to refer to his disciples, both present and future (vv. 2,6,9,11,12,24). Here on the night before going to the cross, Jesus looked back to that time 'before the world was' (v. 5), and that love-gift that the Father had given him. The cross was the means by which the Lord Jesus Christ would redeem those given to him by the Father, and he was obviously ready to go forward.

A third evidence is *his explicit statement*: 'And for their sakes I sanctify myself, that they also may be sanctified by the truth' (v. 19). To 'sanctify' means to set apart, and the Lord Jesus was here expressing his consecration to the task given him.

A final evidence of Jesus' commitment to the cross is *the way he speaks of it as an accomplished reality*: 'I have finished the work which you have given me to do' (v. 4).

As we come away from the account of that memorable night in the upper room, we surely must pause in awe and wonder to contemplate the undiminished faithfulness of Jesus Christ to dying on Calvary's cross to purchase our salvation. He was mere hours away from all its untold anguish and agony, and yet he still embraced it and affirmed it. And he did so out of love for his Father and for those whom the Father had given him.

Deep calls unto deep. It is to the extent that we understand and appreciate his loving faithfulness that we will be lovingly faithful to serve him.

19.
The Son affirms the cross: Gethsemane

Matthew 26:39; Hebrews 5:7

As we have seen in earlier chapters, it was determined in eternity past that the Second Person of the Trinity would take unto himself our humanity and in that humanity would die on the cross. Through that death he would purchase as his own the love-gift the Father promised to give him. That agreement between the three persons of the Trinity established the cross of Christ as the central event of all time. Everything began to look forward to that, and the Son of God began to approach that cross. It was announced there in Eden by God the Father. It was anticipated throughout the entire Old Testament period through various types and through the preaching of the prophets.

Finally, the time arrived for the Son to leave heaven's glory and come to this earth as a mere baby. The angels announced that he had come to be the Saviour. The cross was in view that night in Bethlehem.

The Lord Jesus began his public ministry with the cross very much in view. John the Baptist announced him as the Lamb of God who had come to take away the sin of the world, and Jesus raised no protest. The cross was in view. It was in view when he encountered Satan in the wilderness. The temptation to avoid the cross was dismissed along with Satan himself. Jesus kept that cross in full view all during his public ministry and in his private comments to his disciples. It was definitely before him on the Mount of Transfiguration and during the triumphal entry into Jerusalem. It was still before him there in the upper room as he washed his disciples' feet and offered them words of encouragement and comfort. It was there when he prayed the marvellous prayer of John 17. At each one of these major junctures there was an unruffled calm about Jesus.

Then came Gethsemane, and all that seems to have been in place suddenly appears to go out the window. All that has been nailed down suddenly seems to come loose. Gethsemane seems to be the place where the Lord Jesus Christ threw overboard his firm resolution to go to the cross and made a last-ditch, frantic effort to find a way round it. The whole plan of salvation seems to hang by a mere thread there in Gethsemane as Jesus cries, 'O my Father, if it is possible, let this cup pass from me...' (Matt. 26:39).

The sudden unwillingness of the Saviour seems further to be forced upon us by the way in which the author of Hebrews describes Jesus' experience in Gethsemane: 'In the days of his flesh, when he had offered up prayers and supplications, with vehement cries and tears to him who was able to save him from death...' (Heb. 5:7).

We have already noticed his statement that Satan had nothing in him. But here it seems as if Satan may very well have found something after all, as if there is at last a lack of willingness on Jesus' part to go to the cross. Are these Scriptures telling us that Jesus finally wavered in his determination to go to the cross? Was the salvation provided by Christ's death on the cross the work of a Saviour sullied with reluctance and grudging obedience?

Credit John Flavel with putting the problem succinctly: 'Here is the difficulty, how Christ, who knew God had from everlasting determined he should drink it, who had compacted and agreed with him in the covenant of redemption so to do, who came (as himself acknowledges) for that end into the world ... who foresaw this hour all along, and professed when he spake of this bloody baptism with which he was to be baptized, that he was "straitened till it was accomplished"... How (I say) to reconcile all this with such a petition, that now when the cup was delivered to him, it might pass, or he excused from suffering; this is the knot, this is the difficulty.'[1]

When we tiptoe into Gethsemane to hear the Saviour's anguished pleas, we must recognize we are entering the realm of infinities and immensities. We are out of our element here. No mere human analysis will ever be able to explain fully the awesome dimensions of what took place there. Here the Son of God approaches God the Father. The Son of God makes this approach as one who is fully divine and fully human. Furthermore, the Son of God makes this approach only hours before carrying out the plan formalized in eternity past. Who can understand such things? We must content ourselves with a faint insight or two into the blackness of Gethsemane.

The fact that we cannot understand everything about Gethsemane does not mean we cannot understand anything at all. We are able to penetrate some of its mysteries by keeping in mind a couple of things.

Jesus fulfils a requirement for his mission

The first of these is that Gethsemane was not an aberration in the plan of salvation. It was not a temporary detour down a side-street on the road to redemption. The plan of salvation did not precariously hang by a single thread there. Gethsemane was part and parcel of the plan of redemption.

In Gethsemane we see the Saviour doing something that had to be done in order to be our Saviour. The author of Hebrews, in writing about Christ as our High Priest, says Gethsemane was the means of perfecting Christ. He puts it in these words: 'And having been perfected, he became the author of eternal salvation to all who obey him' (Heb. 5:9).

That word 'perfected' does not imply that Jesus was morally imperfect or deficient. It refers to being fitted or qualified for a task. What was the task Jesus had to be fitted for? The task of being our High Priest. What was the work of the high priest? It was to make atonement for the sins of people, to represent sinners before God. What was necessary for someone to be a high priest? He had to be one of those he was representing. He had to partake of human nature himself; he had to have a bond, a sympathy, with those he was representing.

In Gethsemane the Lord Jesus Christ was fitted to be our High Priest. There we see him descending, as it were, the steep slope of complete identification with those he came to save. There he already began to feel the pangs of damnation their depravity deserved. There he began to experience the reality of being forsaken by God. And there, in his full identification with us, he cried out, as any of the damned would do, 'Let this cup pass!' He had to desire, in his human nature, the cup of God's wrath against sin to pass, or he could not have been identified with us.

The author of Hebrews makes this clear in these words: 'For we do not have a High Priest who cannot sympathize with our weaknesses, but was in all points tempted as we are, yet without sin' (Heb. 4:15). And when he came away from it all, it was as one who could represent his people because he had fully and completely experienced their condemnation, and cried their cry.

Jesus demonstrates the fulness of his humanity

This is not to say that our Lord was putting on an act in Gethsemane. His humanity was a real humanity, and in that humanity he truly felt the anguish and the pain of the cross. It was that humanity that shrank from the cross and longed to have it removed.

The distinction we must make is between the two natures of Christ. He was fully God and fully man. We can say, therefore, that Jesus embraced the cross with his divine nature, while shrinking from it with his human nature.

William Hendriksen expresses this view in these words: 'Never shall we, who do not even know how our own soul and body interact, be able to grasp how the human nature of Christ, in these solemn moments, related itself toward the divine, or vice versa. To the intense suffering, experienced in Christ's human nature, was given infinite value by means of the union of this human to the divine nature, within the second person of the Holy Trinity.'[2]

John Gill says of Christ's experience in Gethsemane, 'That there are two wills in Christ, human and divine, is certain; his human will, though in some instances, as in this, may have been different from the divine will, yet not contrary to it; and his divine will is always the same with his Father's. This, as mediator, he engaged to do, and came down from heaven for that purpose, took delight in doing it, and has completely finished it.'[3]

The Lord Jesus himself seems to have suggested this in his words to his sleeping disciples: 'The spirit indeed is willing, but the flesh is weak' (Matt. 26:41).

Jesus was struggling with his flesh in Gethsemane. S. G. DeGraaf neatly captures the significance of Christ's struggle by saying, '"Flesh" here does not mean man in his sin, because Jesus had so sin, but man in his weakness. The weakness, of course, is the result of sin but is not the sin itself.'[4]

But why did Jesus struggle so with his flesh? It was more than just the prospect of death. Many have faced death with a substantial degree of calmness. It was not the idea of death itself that caused Jesus to be 'sorrowful and deeply distressed' (Matt. 26:37). It was rather the nature of that approaching death.

F. B. Meyer writes of Jesus, 'He knew that he was about to be brought into the closest association with the sin which was devastating human happiness and grieving the divine nature. He knew, since He had so identified Himself with our fallen race, that, in a very deep and wonderful way, He was to be made sin and to bear our curse and shame, cast out by man, and apparently forsaken by God. He knew as we shall never know, the exceeding sinfulness and horror of sin; and what it was to be the meeting-place where the iniquities of our race should converge, to become the scapegoat charged with guilt not His own, to bear away the sins of the world. All this was beyond measure terrible to one so holy and sensitive as He.'[5]

So the thing Jesus shrank from in Gethsemane was the prospect of being separated from God as he bore the wrath of God against sin. In his spirit he was ready and willing to carry out the plan of redemption, but his flesh revolted at the thought of it.

We know from our own experience that it is possible for us to embrace something with the mind or spirit while shrinking from it with our flesh. Most of us would say this happens when we face surgery, or even a dental appointment. But this was no mere surgery or dental appointment that Jesus was facing! It was the wrath of God against the sins of those whom he had given the Son! We can well understand that Jesus' human nature shrank from that. And we must always remember that the humanity of Jesus was real. It was no mere 'zip-on' humanity.

Our Lord's experience in the garden of Gethsemane is, then, of one piece with the rest of his life and ministry. It was not a last-minute, desperate attempt to persuade the Father to remove the cross. It was the Lord fulfilling another requirement in his mission. As he emerged from Gethsemane it was to say emphatically, 'Shall I not drink the cup which my Father has given me?' (John 18:11).

In his remarkable book, *The Cross He Bore,* Frederick S. Leahy rightly observes: 'In Gethsemane it was never a question whether the Saviour would obey or disobey. In Eden God asked, "Adam, where are you?" In a sense the question was repeated in Gethsemane and this Adam did not try to hide; he had no need to; his whole response was clearly, "Here am I!"'[6]

20.
The Son affirms the cross: from Gethsemane to Golgotha

John 18-19

It might seem as if the Lord Jesus finally ceased affirming the cross when he was at last arrested and taken away, and that he became entirely passive from that moment until he burst from the grave in glorious resurrection life.

There is, of course, a sense in which Jesus was passive during those hours. The prophecy of Isaiah said that he would be 'led as a lamb to the slaughter' and would be as 'a sheep before its shearers' (Isa. 53:7). That is passivity. But we err if we understand Jesus' passivity to be that of a helpless victim. Jesus was passive because he chose to be, not because he had to be. He could at any time have brought the whole process to a speedy end. Each time he refused to do so he mightily affirmed his death on the cross.

Even when it appears as if the Jews were in charge, or Pilate was in charge, or the Romans were in charge, the truth is that Jesus was still in charge. He once said, 'I lay down my life that I may take it again. No one takes it from me, but I lay it down of myself. I have power to lay it down, and I have power to take it again. This command I have received from my Father' (John 10:17-18).

What appears to be weakness in those last few hours before the cross was, then, actually power. It was Jesus exerting his power to lay down his life. We see him exerting the power of restraint so that in a marvellous way men could have their way with him and, at the same time, fulfil the plan of God. That power is manifested at each step of the way — during the arrest itself, during the trials and during the cruel mockery of the soldiers.

The arrest

Jesus accepts Judas' kiss

The first example of Jesus' actively restraining himself occurs when the arresting mob, led by Judas Iscariot, put in an appearance at the garden of Gethsemane.

Jesus knew what was coming. A few hours earlier he had announced to his disciples that one of them would betray him. He had looked at Judas and said, 'What you do, do quickly' (John 13:27). When Judas came towards him, Jesus knew the kiss of betrayal was at hand, but he did not resist it. It was part of the road to the cross.

Jesus rebukes Simon Peter

There in the garden Jesus openly expressed his restraint. When the arresting mob, led by Judas, appeared to arrest Jesus, Simon Peter began to wield his sword and succeeded only in cutting off the ear of a poor servant (who was there, not by choice, but because his master required it). Jesus quickly reattached the ear and rebuked Simon: 'Put your sword in its place, for all who take the sword will perish by the sword. Or do you think that I cannot now pray to my Father, and he will provide me with more than twelve legions of angels?' (Matt. 26:52-53).

Imagine what short work twelve legions of angels would have made of the bloodthirsty mob! But the angels did not come because their Lord and Master did not command them to come. Even though he was facing the unspeakable agony of drinking the cup of God's wrath against sin, he did not issue that command. What incredible restraint!

Jesus is bound

After Jesus healed the ear of the servant, the men who had come to arrest him stepped forward and bound him (John 18:12). And Jesus allowed himself to be bound. He did not have to be bound. When the mob had first arrived in the garden, Jesus had stepped forward to meet them and asked, 'Whom are you seeking?' They had answered, 'Jesus of Nazareth,' and Jesus had responded, 'I am he.' Those words had been enough to make them all draw back and fall to the ground (John 18:4-6). If the mere words of Jesus could flatten a snarling mob, we may rest assured Jesus did not have to be bound.

It is striking that Jesus, in stepping forward and identifying himself, placed himself between his disciples and the mob and said, 'Let these go their way...' (John 18:8). What a glorious picture of the cross! There Jesus stood between his people and the penalty for their sins so they might go free.

The trials

The restraint Jesus exercised in his arrest is also on display in his trials before the Jewish and Roman authorities. At any point in the proceedings, Jesus could have completely confounded his judges and refuted the false charges brought against him, but he only responded when his Messiahship was challenged. Why? These trials were designed by men to issue in the crucifixion of Jesus and that was nothing less than the plan of God the Father. Jesus would not, therefore, do anything to frustrate the plans of the authorities.

Pilate, amazed that Jesus was so unco-operative, thundered, 'Do you not know that I have power to crucify you, and power to release you?' (John 19:10). Pilate knew full well the horrid sufferings involved in death by crucifixion and assumed Jesus would want to do everything possible to avoid it. Little did he know that Jesus was in fact deliberately and consciously co-operating with him and with the Jewish authorities in order to bring that crucifixion about, or that his co-operation with Pilate reflected an even higher level of co-operation — that is, with God the Father.

By the way, while Jesus remained silent in the face of much of what was said to him during these trials, he did not let Pilate's comment pass, but told him, 'You could have no power at all against me unless it had been given you from above' (John 19:11).

The mockery and beating

The restraint shown by Jesus during his arrest and trials is an astonishing thing. What provocation he endured! But the most amazing display of his restraint came when Jesus was handed over to the Roman soldiers.

First came the *scourging*. William Hendriksen describes this punishment in this way: 'The Roman scourge consisted of a short wooden handle to which several thongs were attached, the ends equipped with pieces of lead or brass and with sharply pointed bits of bone. The stripes were laid especially on the victim's back, bared and bent. Generally two men were employed to administer this punishment, one lashing the victim from one side, one from the other side, with the result that the flesh was at times lacerated to such an extent that deep-seated veins and arteries, sometimes even entrails and inner organs, were exposed.'[1] Needless to say, this punishment was so severe that it often caused the victim to die before he could be crucified.

In addition to this, the soldiers repeatedly *struck Jesus in the face* with their fists. Isaiah predicted that this beating would be so severe that those who looked upon the Messiah would be 'astonished' and said that, as a result of his beating, 'His visage was marred more than any man' (Isa. 52:14). This prophecy means that the face of Jesus was so marred and disfigured that he did not even appear to be a man.

Never did anyone face more extreme provocation. Never was there such cruelty. But Jesus endured it, not just as a passive victim, but as one actively pursuing the course assigned to him by God the Father. As he endured this horrible scourging and beating, Jesus fulfilled another of Isaiah's prophecies:

> I gave my back to those who struck me,
> And my cheeks to those who plucked out the beard;
> I did not hide my face from shame and spitting
>
> (Isa. 50:6).

Our Lord could have called it to a halt. He could have destroyed his tormentors with one word. But he actually gave his back to those who scourged him and refused to hide his face from their fists.

The road from Gethsemane to Golgotha was the last leg of that journey that began in eternity past. All that Jesus could have done and refused to do on that last leg constitutes an additional affirmation of the cross and causes us to say with R.C. Trench:

Oh wonderful the wonders left undone!
And scarce less wonderful than those he wrought;
Oh self-restraint, passing all human thought,
To have all power, and be as having none;
Oh self-denying love, which felt alone
For needs of others, never for its own!

Section II
On the cross

The long approach of Jesus to the cross came to an end when rough-hewn Roman soldiers pounded the nails into his hands and feet and hoisted the cross into the air.

Now began the most important hours in all of human history. During those hours the Son carried out what he and the Father had planned before the world began. During that time the Lord Jesus fully satisfied the Father's wrath against those whom the Father had given him and purchased a perfect redemption for all those who believe.

Before they nailed him to the cross, the Roman soldiers offered Jesus gall to drink (Matt. 27:34). This was intended to deaden the pain of the sufferer, but Jesus refused it. He would not allow anything to muddle his thinking or insulate him from the suffering of the cross. His work there required him to be in full possession of his senses. Frederick S. Leahy notes, 'Adam had disobeyed knowingly, with all his senses clear. The "last Adam" must obey willingly and with a clear mind.'[1]

The cup that he would drink from was the one the Father had given him to drink, the cup of wrath against the sinners for whom he was dying. Jesus was still affirming the cross even as it lay there beside him. And he continued to affirm it as he hung there in agony and blood. The so-called 'seven words' he spoke while on the cross prove indisputably his affirmation of the cross. They take us to the heart of his suffering there. They are not just the random babblings of a tortured, disoriented sufferer. Instead these words must be understood in terms of Jesus' conscious and deliberate fulfilment of the role that was assigned to him in eternity — the role of mediator, or surety, for his people.

Go back to that eternal council for a moment. What possessed the Son to agree to serve as the surety for those whom the Father was giving him? Two truths shine out through the mistiness of that council: submission to the Father and love for the people. We see both of those reflected in his words on the cross.

Think again about that eternal council. What was necessary in order for the Son of God to perform the work of redemption? He had to take our humanity and in that humanity bear the penalty of our sin, the penalty of being forsaken by God. His dying words reflect his humanity and his sense that God had forsaken him.

As we look at the seven words Jesus spoke from the cross we will see that they all fit into his mediatorial work in one way or another. They are obviously part of the whole fabric of redemption.

21.
Christ submitting to the Father

Luke 23:33-34,46

It is striking that the very first word Jesus spoke from the cross was 'Father' (Luke 23:34). We shall not fully appreciate this until we give full weight to the context in which it was uttered. Luke introduces it with the words: 'Then Jesus said...' What is the significance of this? When was 'then'?

By using this phrase, Luke underscores for us all the things that had happened to Jesus in the hours that immediately preceded his crucifixion. What solemn, terrible hours they were! Taken into custody in the middle of the night, Jesus was hustled through legal proceedings that were themselves illegal. Once delivered into the hands of a contingent of Roman soldiers, he was mocked, ridiculed, spat upon, flogged until his back was shredded into a bloody, raw mass and crowned with a crown of thorns! He was then prodded and driven through the streets of Jerusalem and up the hill of Golgotha where he was nailed to a cross. When he was firmly fastened to it, it was callously and unfeelingly dropped into the hole that had been prepared for it. Now here he hung, suspended between heaven and earth, with blood streaming down his body, surrounded by a multitude staring and gawking at him, and with every nerve in his body screaming in anguish.

Luke's 'then' captures and comprehends all of these things. After all the humiliation, after all the pain, after all the ridicule,

Jesus spoke, and the first word that fell from his parched, cracked lips was 'Father'.

Jesus uttered the word 'Father' again before he died. The very last statement he made, recorded in Luke 23:46, couples the word 'Father' with the words of the psalmist in Psalm 31:5: 'Into your hands I commend my spirit.'

The first and last sayings of Jesus from the cross begin with the word 'Father'. We might say that word brackets the other words. The word 'Father', always rich in meaning, carries special significance in this context. Here it is a treasure chest packed full of precious truth. Let's seek to open it up a little.

What the word 'Father' tells us about Jesus

An expression of continuing submissiveness

The word 'Father' takes us into the mysterious realm of the relationship between the three persons of the Trinity. God the Father, God the Son and God the Holy Spirit are each fully and equally God. One is not more God than another.

But for the purpose of providing redemption for God's people, these three persons assumed different roles. Theologians sometimes refer to this in terms of the 'economic Trinity'. This assuming of different roles required the Father to be the planner and initiator of redemption, the Son to be the provider of it and the Holy Spirit to be the applier of it.

We have been focusing on the Son's action in providing redemption for his people. We can go further and say that this economic Trinity required him to be submissive to the Father in all things.

We have seen that submissiveness at every stage of the journey. It was there when the Son agreed to be the surety for his people. It was there throughout the long ages when his coming was pictured and anticipated in the Old Testament. It was there when he finally rose from the throne of his glory and stepped into human history as a man. It was there when, as a boy of twelve, the Lord Jesus said to his earthly parents, 'Did you not know that I must be about my Father's business?' (Luke 2:49).

Jesus' submissiveness to his Father was always evident in his public ministry. The Gospel writers tell us that he thanked the Father (Matt. 11:25); that he claimed to be sent by the Father and to do the work of the Father (John 5:36); that he came not to speak his own words but the words of the Father (John 12:50); and that the supreme, driving purpose of his life was to glorify the Father (John 12:28; 14:13).

The Father sent the Lord Jesus into this world for a purpose. He came with a mission that was clearly prescribed and laid out for him by the Father. Jesus carefully and diligently followed his Father's plan. He was able to say, 'For I have come down from heaven, not to do my own will, but the will of him who sent me' (John 6:38). On another occasion, he said, 'I always do those things that please him' (John 8:29).

One aspect of Jesus' submissiveness to the Father was his close, intimate fellowship with God every day of his life — a fellowship that was evidenced by his prayer life.

Luke goes to considerable lengths in his Gospel to show us the vital role prayer played in the life of Jesus. He tells us Jesus prayed at his baptism (3:21), before selecting his disciples (6:12), on the Mount of Transfiguration (9:28-29) and on the night before he was crucified (22:41,44). He also tells us Jesus 'often withdrew into the wilderness and prayed' (5:16).

That submissiveness to the Father, ever in place from eternity past, came to its highest expression when Jesus went to the cross.

An expression of affection and trust

In the midst of the most horrifying circumstances imaginable, Jesus could still call God 'Father'.

The night before he was crucified the Lord Jesus had asked the Father to remove the cup of suffering he was experiencing there on the cross. The Father had not removed it, and now Jesus was already drinking the first bitter dregs of that awful cup. He hung there with the full awareness and knowledge that the Father in heaven could have prevented it all and could even now intervene on his behalf. But his faith in God and love for God were still intact.

What the word 'Father' tells us about ourselves

Let's now turn our attention to the lessons we can learn from this prayer.

Having God as Father

The first of these lessons has to do with having God as our Father. We cannot, of course, have God as our Father in exactly the same way Jesus did. He was, and is, the eternal Son of God. But the glory of the Christian message is that we can still have God as our Father. We can know God in a personal, intimate way through the Lord Jesus Christ.

There are many who object to this. Their viewpoint is that God is already the Father of us all, but it only takes a quick glance at the Scriptures to see the fallacy of this view. In John's Gospel we read, 'But as many as received him, to them he gave the right to become children of God, even to those who believe in his name' (John 1:12). Who are those who may be called the children of God? Is it everyone without exception? John affirms that the children of God are those who have received Christ by believing in his name.

Other verses are equally plain on this matter. Once Jesus got into a fiery debate with the Pharisees on this matter of fatherhood. They didn't hesitate to claim God as their Father, but Jesus refused to allow them to get away with it. He said to them, 'If God were your Father, you would love me, for I proceeded forth and came from God, nor have I come of myself [i.e. on my own initiative], but he sent me' (John 8:42).

Having God as our Father is not, then, something that happens to us automatically. We do not have God as our Father simply because we breathe his air. He is only the Father of those who have committed their lives to the redeeming work of his Son, Jesus Christ.

Praying to God as Father

Secondly, we should learn to pray. If Jesus felt the need to pray, how much more should we! In addition to praying himself, Jesus taught his disciples to pray. His parable of the persistent widow was intended to drive home the point that 'Men always ought to pray and not lose heart' (Luke 18:1).

Working for the Father

The second time Jesus used the word 'Father' on the cross was in connection with his committing his spirit to God. And that committal came immediately after he said, 'It is finished.' In other words, Jesus committed himself to the Father only after completing the work assigned to him by the Father.

The same God who sent Jesus into this world for a specific purpose and work has also given all those of us who know

Christ a work to do. We are called to live for his honour and his glory, to show forth his praises and to demonstrate the difference the gospel makes (1 Peter 2:9-10).

We are to be fulfilling this purpose in our families, in our jobs, in our communities. Wherever we are and whatever we do, we are to be conscious of the fact that we belong to God and that we are to live for God. How are we doing with this? Because we are fallible and frail, we cannot perfectly fulfil our purpose as the Lord Jesus did, but we can be diligently working at it.

We may rest assured that death will be far more comfortable for that child of God who has diligently tried to fulfil God's purpose for his or her life. A spiritual principle comes into play here. Those who sow bountifully reap bountifully and those who sow sparingly reap sparingly (2 Cor. 9:6). If we bountifully seek to fulfil God's purpose for our lives we may legitimately expect to find bountiful comfort in the hour of death. On the other hand, if we go sparingly about the Lord's work we can expect to reap a meagre harvest of comfort and grace in the hour of death.

A popular poster reads, 'The Lord has given me a certain number of things to accomplish. At this moment, I am so far behind I will never die.' The truth is, however, that we must die whether our tasks are finished or not. It must be a tremendous sorrow to arrive at the point of death with unfinished business — deeds of kindness left undone, words of love left unspoken, children left untaught in the things of God.

We would do well, then, to heed the challenging words of Charles Spurgeon: 'As long as there is breath in our bodies, let us serve Christ; as long as we can think, as long as we can speak, as long as we can work, let us serve him, let us serve him with our last gasp; and, if it be possible, let us try to get some work going that will glorify him when we are dead and gone.'[1]

Trusting God as Father

In life. We should learn to love and trust God, no matter how difficult our circumstances may be. When we are angry over bitter and adverse circumstances that have come our way, we can learn from the Lord Jesus Christ on the cross to trust God in the midst of difficulty and searing trial. By looking to Jesus' example we can learn to say with the hymn-writer:

> When darkness seems to hide his face,
> I rest on his unchanging grace.
> When all around my soul gives way
> He then is all my hope and stay.
>
> (Edward Mote)

In death. It occurs to me that in one sense Jesus died a very comfortable death. No, of course I am not suggesting there was no pain or anguish in his death. We have noted again and again the terrible suffering through which he went on the cross. I am talking rather about his attitude about death. His final words reveal that he died with strong confidence and without fear and trembling. He speaks of death in terms of placing himself in his Father's hands. These words picture someone depositing something that is very sacred and precious for safe keeping with one who is unquestionably trustworthy.

Would we know how to die? There is no better teacher than the Lord Jesus Christ. No one died more peacefully than he. We can die peacefully as well if we have the confidence that at death our souls go immediately into the hands of the heavenly Father.

Jesus had been in the hands of wicked people. The Bible emphasizes this in verse after verse. In Matthew 17:22-23 Jesus predicted his death in these words: 'The Son of Man is about to be betrayed into the hands of men, and they will kill him...' He repeated the same thing minutes before he was taken into custody (Matt. 26:45). Other verses also make reference to Jesus being in the hands of wicked men (Luke 24:6-7; Acts 2:23).

As Jesus came to the point of death, he knew he was no longer in the hands of men. Their hands had done all they could do to him, and now he could commit himself to the hands of his Father. Do we understand the implications of this? Jesus knew his soul was going to be received by the Father at the very moment of death. His body was, of course, to be placed in a tomb and resurrected on the third day. At the time of his resurrection his soul and body were reunited, but his soul was safe in the Father's hands during the time his body was entombed.

It is exactly the same for the one who knows God as Father. At the point of death, his soul goes immediately into God's presence and there remains until his body is raised from the grave. At that time his soul and body will be reunited and he will go to live for ever with the Lord (1 Thess. 4:13-18), and there he finally will be free from all the wicked hands that have mistreated and abused him here.

How this takes the sting out of death for the Christian! Tell him that death is going to come to him before the day is over, and he will rejoice with the knowledge that for the Christian to be absent from the body is to be present with the Lord (2 Cor. 5:6-8). This makes death a promotion and not a tragedy, and those who grieve over a Christian grieve for themselves and their loss. John Bunyan understood this. In the *Pilgrim's Progress*, when Christiana died, Bunyan says her children wept, but Mr Great-heart and Mr Valiant, two men of faith who knew what death was about, 'played upon the well-tuned cymbal and harp for joy'.[2]

The unbeliever has no such comfort. Yes, there is a set of hands ready to receive him in the hour of death, but they are not the hands of a loving, heavenly Father. They are the fiery hands of Satan himself who eagerly clutches at his prey to pull it down into eternal destruction.

There is, then, a set of hands to receive each and every one of us when we come to the hour of death. The question is only which set of hands it will be.

22.
Christ loving sinners

Luke 23:34,43

Jesus was a man of two constant, unyielding principles. The first is conveyed to us by the word 'Father'. He loved the Father, submitted to him and communed with him. That principle was in place in eternity past and continued to be in place until the work of redemption was done. There was not so much as a single wavering or let-up in it.

For the second of these principles, we must return to the first words he spoke from the cross and go beyond them to include the second time he spoke. Each of these sayings reveals Christ's love for sinners. Just as the Son's submissiveness to the Father was in place before the world began, so was his love for sinners. The Father's gift of love to the Son consisted of a humanity that lay in the dunghill of sin, a humanity the Son would have to redeem before it could be his. The Son could have refused such a gift, but he did not. His heart went out in love for those ruined and devastated by sin. There in eternity — astonishing thought — he set his heart upon guilty sinners.

The flame of that eternal love burned brightly and undiminished through all those centuries in which the Son's redeeming work was anticipated and throughout his public ministry. But it was never more apparent than when Jesus was on the cross. There he prayed for sinners, and there he made a promise to a sinner and, in doing so, left us two of the most cheering words in all of history.

'Forgive them...'

The first words of Jesus from the cross were a prayer. We might expect to read that he prayed, 'Father, help me.' Many people enter the dark recesses of death with this petition upon their lips, but not Jesus.

Given the cruel circumstances of his death, we might have expected him to pray, 'Father, consume these people who are crucifying me.' But neither did he ask for that. Instead he prayed, 'Father, forgive them, for they do not know what they do.'

In his Sermon on the Mount, Jesus had said to his disciples, 'Love your enemies, bless those who curse you, do good to those who hate you, and pray for those who spitefully use you and persecute you' (Matt. 5:44). These first words from the cross reveal that our Lord Jesus practised the very same thing he had preached.

For whom was he praying? The ones around the cross of whom it could most truly be said that they did not know what they were doing were the Roman soldiers. Caught up in the business at hand, they were completely oblivious to the eternal realities being played out before their very eyes. They were truly ignorant of what they were doing. The religious leaders, on the other hand, had brazenly turned their backs on a massive amount of evidence that Jesus was indeed the Messiah, evidence the poor soldiers were blissfully unaware of.

By asking God to forgive these people, Jesus was saying, in the words of William Hendriksen, 'Blot out their transgression completely. In thy sovereign grace cause them to repent truly, so that they can be and will be pardoned fully.'[1]

No, Jesus was not excusing their sin. Ignorance does not excuse us for breaking God's law. But Jesus was describing their condition. Sin does indeed blind us. It had blinded these soldiers to the person of Christ and to the enormity of their sin, and it does the same for us. But, thank God, Jesus cares for poor, blind, ignorant sinners! He takes no delight in sinners perishing. He came to seek and to save sinners (Luke 19:10).

This prayer was abundantly answered. Even before the body of Jesus was removed from the cross, this prayer began to be answered. The centurion witnessed Jesus take his last breath and exclaimed, 'Truly this man was the Son of God!' (Mark 15:39). The Gospel of Matthew tells us the soldiers who were with him joined in this assessment (Matt. 27:54). Some argue that this was not a full-fledged confession of faith, that the centurion and his soldiers were only convinced that Jesus was an unusual man — indeed, a man of God. I cannot help but think, however, that the death of Christ, which was for the express purpose of redeeming lost souls, should have immediately had that effect.

Even many of the religious leaders themselves came to embrace Jesus as the Christ. Fifty days after the resurrection of Jesus, the apostle Peter stood to preach in Jerusalem. Many in his audience that day had witnessed the crucifixion, and Peter did not hesitate to confront them with the wickedness of it all and to call them to repentance. Many of them did not realize until that moment that they had actually been a party to crucifying the very Son of God. But as Peter preached their hearts were pierced with the truth. On that day alone, many of the people responsible for crucifying the Lord Jesus repented of their sins and received him as their Lord and Saviour (Acts 2:36-37).

The great preacher of the nineteenth century, Charles Spurgeon, looks at Jesus' prayer for forgiveness in a slightly different way. He says, 'I love this prayer ... because of the indistinctness of it. It is "Father, forgive them." He does not say, "Father, forgive the soldiers who have nailed me here." He includes them. Neither does he say, "Father, forgive the people who are beholding me." He means them. Neither does he say, "Father, forgive sinners in ages to come who will sin against me." But he means them. Jesus does not mention them by any accusing name: "Father, forgive my enemies. Father, forgive my murderers." No, there is no word of accusation upon those dear lips. "Father, forgive them." Now into that pronoun "them" I feel that I can crawl. Can you get in there? Oh, by a humble faith, appropriate the cross of Christ by trusting in it; and get into that big little word "them"! It seems like a chariot of mercy that has come down to earth, into which a man may step and it shall bear him up to heaven.[2]

Spurgeon's words remind me of the story of the little boy who was angry with his mother. When he knelt beside his bed for his bedtime prayer, he asked God to bless every member of his family except his mother. When he crawled into bed, he looked at his mother and said, 'I suppose you noticed you were not in it.'[3] Thank God, as Spurgeon points out, that 'them' in Jesus' prayer is large enough to include all who want God's forgiveness.

'Teacher, which is the greatest commandment in the law?' That was the question put to Jesus by a lawyer just a few days before the crucifixion. Jesus responded, '"You shall love the Lord your God with all your heart, with all your soul, and with all your mind." This is the first and great commandment. And the second is like it: "You shall love your neighbour as yourself"' (Matt. 22:36-39).

In saying 'Father', Jesus showed he was keeping the first and greatest commandment. In saying 'forgive them', he showed he was keeping the second greatest commandment. In other words, Jesus died as he lived — with a heart filled with devotion to God and love for his fellow man.

'Today you will be with me in paradise'

Jesus was crucified between two thieves. The religious leaders of the day probably derived no small delight from this. To them it was the ultimate insult to the one they despised so much. The self-proclaimed Messiah dying with common criminals — what more proof could there be that he was an impostor? But what they regarded as proof of their position was just the opposite. The prophet Isaiah had predicted that the Messiah would be 'numbered with the transgressors' in his death (Isa. 53:12).

The first time Jesus spoke on the cross, he prayed. The second time he answered the prayer of one of the thieves. After initially joining in the mockery and ridicule that others were heaping upon Jesus, this one thief suddenly stopped and offered this prayer: 'Lord, remember me when you come into your kingdom.' Jesus answered that prayer by assuring this thief that the two of them would be together in paradise that very day.

The words Jesus spoke to this thief have consoled and comforted countless numbers down through the course of the centuries. The dying words of Jesus have proved to be undying.

The man to whom these words were spoken

Consider the man to whom these words were spoken. It should be apparent to us that he was *a very wicked man.* By his own admission (v. 41), he was a malefactor, a criminal. He was a thief and, according to some, a murderer.

The Lord Jesus Christ was dying the death of a criminal, but he was innocent. This man was dying the death of a criminal because he was a criminal. The fact that Jesus spoke so kindly and generously to such a man ought to fill our hearts with joy.

No matter how great our wickedness, we can come to Christ and find mercy and grace.

We must also remember that this man was *dying*. His wasted life was quickly drawing to a close. His life's blood was rapidly seeping out of his tortured body and falling to the ground beneath. Hell's mouth was yawning to receive his soul.

We have in this man an accurate description of ourselves. We are all wicked and we are all dying. Do you object to this? Many do. They protest in words like these: 'Hold on a minute! I'm not perfect, but I'm certainly not like this thief. I have never stolen anything. I am a respectable, law-abiding citizen.' They fail to realize that it is entirely possible to be perfectly respectable in their own eyes and in the eyes of those around them. But what about God's eyes? Those prying eyes see every crevice, every nook and cranny of your heart. They never close in sleep, and they are never diverted by distractions. Those eyes can see stealing when no one else can. God demands that we love him with all our heart, mind, soul and strength. Have we given this to God, or have we taken it from him and given it to another? Alas, we are all thieves after all. And this one who can see stealing when we can't also sees every other form of sin in our hearts and lives. This great, all-seeing one says of us, 'There is none righteous, no, not one' (Rom. 3:10).

The wickedness of man is written so large and so clearly in our society and in our own lives that one can only be amazed that any should dispute it. However, it is beyond dispute that we are dying. The grim reaper steadily swings his scythe and all die, whether they be rich or poor, educated or illiterate, powerful or weak.

Why is it so important for us to take our place alongside this thief as wicked, dying people? Because it is only as we occupy his place that we are in a position to receive his blessing. What was his blessing? Hearing the words of Jesus: 'Today you will be with me in paradise.' Those words were spoken to a wicked, dying man, and we may take them for ourselves if we will admit that we are wicked, dying people.

The truths these words unveil

That brings us to consider what these words tell us.

1. A glorious place. First, they tell us there is a glorious state, a glorious condition, beyond this life. Jesus here calls it 'paradise'. What was he referring to? Only on two other occasions do we find this word used in Scripture (2 Cor. 12:4; Rev. 2:7), and in each case it is used as a synonym for heaven.

Jesus was, therefore, promising life in heaven to this thief, and this promise was going to be fulfilled that very day. The moment that the thief died his soul went immediately into the presence of God. His body was, of course, taken down from the cross and, we presume, buried. When the Lord Jesus Christ comes again, that body will be raised from the grave and will be reunited with his soul, but his soul joined God in heaven on the day he died. It remains in heaven today, and it will remain there until the day of the resurrection.

What a glorious thought is heaven! And we may rest assured that our highest flights of imagination fall far short of the reality. It is the place of no tears, no sorrow, no pain, no death and no parting. Isn't it amazing that so few are interested in this place and how to get there?

2. The one who has the keys. The second thing the words of Jesus tell us is that he is the one who has the keys to heaven.

The thief called him 'Lord'. Here was Jesus, dying on a cross, and this man called him 'Lord'. He did not look like God in human flesh at that point, but the Spirit of God had so worked faith in the heart of this dying thief that he was able to look beyond outward appearances to see the reality of who Jesus was. So it is today. When the Spirit of God works faith in a person's heart he enables that person to see what others cannot see.

Notice that Jesus did not dispute what the man had said, or correct him. When this man called him 'Lord', Jesus simply responded in lordly fashion by saying, 'I say to you…' In other words, he accepted the title the thief used for him.

Now the point is that if Jesus is Lord, he has supreme authority over all, including entrance to paradise.

3. How heaven's door swings open. The third thing the words of Jesus tell us is what we must do if we want the Lord to open heaven's door to us.

Let's not forget that Jesus spoke these words in response to what this thief had prayed. And what did this thief's prayer include? It contains, in the words of one commentator, 'a very large and long creed'.[4] In effect, the thief said the following in his prayer: 'I am a sinful man. I deserve the punishment placed upon me. This man, on the other hand, is pure and righteous. I will, therefore, trust him and him alone for my salvation.'

If we would have heaven's door swing open to us so that we may enter paradise, we must make the prayer of this thief ours. We must stop arguing with God and start agreeing with him. We must say the same thing about ourselves that he says about us — namely, that we are indeed sinners and deserve only his eternal wrath. We must further recognize that we can do no more to help ourselves than this thief could do. We must see that Jesus Christ is our only hope for salvation and cast ourselves entirely on his mercy and grace.

4. A sombre reality. The final thing the words of the Lord tell us is very sombre indeed — all will not make it to heaven.

Jesus spoke these words to one thief, and to one thief alone. The other thief refused to cast himself upon the mercy of the Lord. His prayer was, 'Save yourself and us.' He was concerned only with what Jesus could do for him in this life. He could not see as far as the life beyond. How many today are like him! Their only interest is in a God who helps them with this short span. Speak to them about a God who will help them for eternity, and they turn quickly away.

It was no accident that Jesus' cross was placed between the two thieves. He is the great divider of men. Those who receive him are saved; those who reject him are lost for ever. Those two thieves, one on Jesus' right and the other on his left, are not only fitting symbols for all humanity this very day, but they are also fitting symbols for that future Day of Judgement when his sheep will be placed on his right and the goats will be placed on his left and driven away for ever. Those who go through life on the wrong side of Christ will certainly find themselves on the wrong side of him in eternity.

23.
Christ loving his own

John 19:25-27

The first two sayings of Jesus from the cross reveal his heart of love for sinners. The third reveals his heart of love for those who have already come to know him. The people of God are always divided into two groups: those who have not yet come to know Christ and those who have. The love of Christ goes out to each of these.

Who can comprehend the tender love Christ has for his own? The apostle John, in his introduction to the account of the night before Jesus was crucified, gives us a glimpse of that love with these words: 'Now before the feast of the Passover, when Jesus knew that his hour had come that he should depart from this world to the Father, having loved his own who were in the world, he loved them to the end' (John 13:1).

It would have been a marvel if Jesus had felt even a fleeting compassion for anyone in this world of sin. But Jesus did not just feel a fleeting compassion for one person. He had an abiding love for the many whom John refers to as 'his own'.

John gives us another glimpse into the love of Christ for his own as he tells us of the third time Jesus spoke from the cross: 'Now there stood by the cross of Jesus his mother...' (v. 25). Are there any words more heart-rending than these? Jesus was dying the most horrid, ignominious death possible and his mother was there to see it. She heard the hammer blows that drove the nails and must have winced with each blow. She saw the cruel cross lifted in the air and heard his cry of pain as it was dropped abruptly into the ground. She saw the blood flowing down. She heard the mockery and ridicule of the gloating religious leaders and the others around the cross. She heard the callous cursing and laughing of the soldiers as they went about their grim business.

Shortly after Jesus was born that old saint of God, Simeon, had looked deep into Mary's eyes and solemnly said, 'Yes, a sword will pierce through your own soul also...' (Luke 2:35). There in the shadow of the cross, Mary felt the thrust of that sword. Never were a more gruesome death and a more gracious Son joined than here.

The other women gathered there around the cross had probably tried to persuade her to stay away from the savage spectacle, but she was inexorably drawn there by one of the strongest forces known to man — a mother's love. 'Many waters cannot quench love, nor can the floods drown it' (S. of S. 8:7).

We are blessed when the trials of life swell up around us if we have faithful friends on whom we can depend to the very end. These Mary had. Her sister was there and Mary Magdalene, that woman who owed such a massive debt to grace, was there. And one of the twelve, John, was there.

All of Jesus' disciples had forsaken him and fled, but John had returned. John consistently identifies himself in his Gospel as 'the disciple whom Jesus loved'. Perhaps that phrase carries with it the reason why he thought better of his cowardice and returned to take his place at the foot of the cross. The glory of his life was in being embraced by the love of Christ. No, he did not glory in his love for Christ. It was too weak and faltering. But the love of Christ for him — that must have been the invisible hand that pulled him back to his rightful place. If we are to shun cowardice and stand with Christ as John did, we must dwell much on the Christ who loved us and gave himself for us.

That little company of believers must have felt very much alone there on that barren Golgotha. They were a tiny island of love and devotion in a sea of hatred and disdain. They were a tiny patch of blue in a sullen, grey sky. They were a spray of tender flowers in the midst of a tangle of thorns and brambles. Suddenly Jesus looked upon that little company and spoke to his mother: 'Woman, behold your son!' He must have nodded towards John as he spoke those words. And then to John he said, 'Behold your mother!' and nodded towards Mary.

These few words carried a world of meaning for Mary, and they contain powerful and large lessons for us.

Jesus' tender concern for the needs of this life

First, they show us the tender concern of the Lord Jesus for those who have pressing, urgent needs in this life. Mary had such needs. The future must have looked very bleak to her as she stood there watching her son die. Her husband had died. Her other sons had still not accepted Jesus as the Messiah, and she probably could not count on them for either physical or emotional support. And now Jesus was being taken from her.

What was to become of her? Jesus' words gave the answer. With those words he placed Mary in John's care and charged John to treat her as though she were his own mother. His words found their mark for the next thing we read is, 'From that hour that disciple took her to his own home.' So Jesus was not so occupied with his own needs that he neglected the needs of his mother. He saw to it that she was cared for before he died.

Concern for others was always to the forefront of Jesus' life. And now it is to the forefront in his death. The first three sayings of Jesus on the cross were spoken on behalf of others.

This is not surprising. The whole purpose of Jesus' death was to help others. He did not have to die. No Roman nails were strong enough to hold him to that cross. He died for our sake, and the nails that held him there were the nails of love. He was there to act as our High Priest, to make an atonement for sin and to offer it to God on the behalf of his people.

There are a couple of things for us to learn from Jesus' concern for the needs of others. First, if Jesus is so deeply concerned about our needs, we can and should bring our needs to him. What troubles you today? Have friends turned against you? Do you carry serious illness in your body? Are you lonely and depressed? No matter what your problem is and no matter how overwhelming it is, there are two things you should do. First, think long and hard on these precious words from the author of Hebrews: 'For we do not have a High Priest who cannot sympathize with our weaknesses' (Heb. 4:15). Then do as the hymn-writer says and take your burden to Jesus:

> I must tell Jesus all of my trials;
> I cannot bear these burdens alone;
> In my distress he kindly will help me;
> He ever loves and cares for his own.
>
> (Elisha A. Hoffman)

Thank God, we can bring our burdens to Jesus with the confidence that he cares about us and will help us. That does not necessarily mean he will remove the burden from us, but if he does not we may rest assured it is because the burden is for our good and he will give us strength and grace to bear it.

Jesus' concern for the needs of others teaches another lesson as well. If our Lord was so concerned about others, his followers should also be concerned about others. Have we learned this lesson from our Lord? Or have we bought into the self-centredness of our day, with its emphasis on 'my needs'?

How much do we really live for others and care for their needs? Their own needs, problems, wants, circumstances and disappointments make up the whole of reality as far as many are concerned.

Let's see to it that we never forget that our family members are included in that category of others. All too often we treat the worst those we profess to love the most. In particular, let's make sure we obey God's clear command to honour our parents. If Jesus had time in the midst of dying to respect his mother, we can surely find time in the midst of living to respect our parents. What does it mean to honour our parents? It means giving them obedience in our younger years, support in their older years and respect through all their years.

The priority of the next life

The second significant lesson these words teach us is the priority Jesus gives to preparing for the next life.

This lesson comes out in a couple of ways. First, the fact that Jesus was concerned about Mary and her physical needs did not cause him to come down from the cross and abandon the work of redemption he was performing there. He could have done this. He did not have to stay on the cross. He could have put Mary's physical needs above everything else and come down from the cross, but he did not. Instead he gave priority to opening the door of heaven to all who believe in him.

The second indication that Jesus gave priority to the next life arises from the way in which he addressed Mary. He did not address her as 'mother', but simply as 'woman'. Many have found this disturbing. It appears to them that Jesus was being rude and inconsiderate. Nothing could be further from the truth. Jesus addressed Mary as 'woman', not to be rude but to underscore a most vital truth — namely, that their relationship was now changed for ever. Herschel Ford explains it in this way: 'On the Cross Jesus actually broke the relationship of mother and son. He turned her away from Himself by saying, "From now on not I, but John, is to be your son." From that time He is no longer anyone's son — He is the world's Saviour. Mary no longer is the mother, she is a simple believer, and her Son has become her Saviour... He provided for her as a Saviour a million times better home than He provided for her as a son.'[1]

F. W. Krummacher makes the same point in these words: 'His earthly connection with her must give way to a superior one. As though He had said, "Thou, My mother, wilt from this time be as one of My daughters, and I thy Lord... The relationships according to the flesh and the manner of the world have an end; other and more spiritual and heavenly take their place."'[2]

It is surely no accident that we find Jesus using the same form of address for Mary on another occasion when he was much occupied with the work of the cross (John 2:4). While Jesus was concerned about Mary's physical needs, he was even more concerned about carrying out the work of providing eternal salvation for sinners. The needs of this life pale in comparison to that.

Have you received the eternal life Jesus came to provide? Many seem only to be interested in the Christ who meets the physical needs. They want a God who cares about them in the here and now and who helps them with the problems of this life, but they disdain the eternal salvation he offers. They want to accept the lesser gift of his caring concern for the problems of this life and reject the greater gift of eternal life. The tragedy is that they can have both.

24.
Christ performing the task

Matthew 27:45-46

Jesus was nailed to the cross at nine in the morning. He died at three in the afternoon. The first three of his dying words were spoken during his first three hours on the cross. The last four were uttered in quick succession just before he died at three.

From noon till three Jesus said nothing. These were the hours when darkness fell over the land, the hours at which the sun normally shines its brightest. These hours were, in the words of William Hendriksen, 'intense and unforgettable'.[1]

Thomas Manton says, 'The sun seemed to be struck blind with astonishment, and the frame of nature to put itself into a funeral garb and habit, as if the creatures durst not show their glory while … Christ was suffering.'[2]

Perhaps Charles Spurgeon put it best: 'It was midnight at midday.'[3] Never has there been such darkness. When Jesus was born a brilliant burst of light bathed the fields around Bethlehem (Luke 2:9), but at his death there was no light — only the deepest darkness.

After those three long hours of darkness, Jesus spoke again: 'My God, my God, why have you forsaken me?' This is the fourth saying from the cross with three on each side of it. It is, therefore, the central word, and that is singularly appropriate because it brings us to the very heart of what Jesus' death was

all about. This was his own explanation of those hours of
darkness. They were hours in which God withdrew from him
and turned his back on him. During that period of time Jesus
was deprived of fellowship and communion with God.

Now we can understand why a thick veil of darkness was
drawn around the land at the time of the crucifixion. It was a
visible and outward manifestation of God's withdrawal from
Jesus. The Bible says, 'God is light' (1 John 1:5). So if God
withdrew from Jesus, darkness would be fitting.

The great withdrawal

But why should God withdraw from Jesus? That is the key
question. If we are to understand this amazing fact, we must
address the problem the cross was designed to deal with.

There are two parts to this problem. One part is man's sin;
the other is God's holiness. There should be no debate about
the first of these. The truth of it is written too large across our
society to dispute.

Many are quick to acknowledge the fact of sin, but they fail
to understand the seriousness of it. Sin would not be so serious
if we simply had to answer to each other. One sinner would be
inclined to overlook the failings of another sinner. But we do
not have to answer to each other; we have to answer to God.
The Bible says we must all stand before him and give account
of ourselves (Rom. 14:12).

Can we now see how serious sin is? The one before whom
we must stand and give account is holy. That means he simply
cannot ignore our sin, or pretend that it never took place. If he
did that he would be denying and compromising his holy
nature. The prophet Habakkuk states it graphically when he
says to God, 'You are of purer eyes than to behold evil, and
cannot look on wickedness' (Hab. 1:13).

God's nature requires him, therefore, to judge sin. And he has already pronounced judgement upon it. What is the penalty God has pronounced upon sin? It is eternal separation from him and from everything that is good. This penalty comes out clearly in a couple of verses. In Matthew 25:41 we find that God will say to all those who appear before him in their sins, 'Depart from me, you cursed, into the everlasting fire prepared for the devil and his angels.'

The apostle Paul has this to say about those who appear before God with their sins unforgiven: 'These shall be punished with everlasting destruction from the presence of the Lord and from the glory of his power' (2 Thess. 1:9).

Note the link between sin and separation in these verses. One says God will send the wicked away with the solemn word, 'Depart'. The other speaks of being away 'from the presence of the Lord'. Sin separates us from fellowship and communion with God in this life, and it finally culminates in eternal separation. If something is not done about our sin, eternal separation from God will be our lot. This separation from God is what hell is all about.

But there is even more to God's withdrawal from Jesus than that. It is not only that God's holiness compels him to banish sin from his presence, but it also requires him actively to judge sin. The Father's withdrawal from Christ on the cross was also, then, an expression of the Father's active penal wrath against the sin Christ was bearing there on the cross. In other words, it is not just that sin is so repulsive to God that he will not be in its presence, but also it is so offensive to him that his wrath is kindled against it.

All of this can all be placed in the category of bad news but, thank God, there is also good news. This holy God who has pronounced the penalty of eternal separation upon sin has done what was necessary for our sins to be forgiven and its penalty to be lifted.

What did he do? He sent his Son, the Lord Jesus Christ, into this world to take the penalty for sinners upon himself. Jesus was qualified to do this in two ways. First, he lived a perfect life and had, therefore, no sin of his own to pay for. This means he could pay for the sins of someone else. In addition to that, he was God in human flesh and, as an infinite person, he could pay for the sins of more than one.

Are you beginning to see how the cross deals with the problem of sin? Sin has to be punished. God's holiness demands that. And yet God's love demands that the sinner go free. Through the death of Jesus on the cross, God satisfied both the demands of his justice and love. Justice was satisfied in that sin was punished in Jesus, and love was satisfied because, since Jesus took on himself the penalty for sin, there is no penalty left for the sinner to pay.

The meaning of the cross is this: Jesus took the penalty for sinners so they do not have to pay that penalty themselves. Is the penalty for sin separation from God? What, then, did Jesus have to do in order to pay it? He had to be separated from God. Is separation from God the same as hell? Then when Jesus was separated from God on the cross, he was enduring the very pangs of hell itself.

This is what his cry was all about. During those three hours of darkness, Jesus was experiencing in his soul the penalty on behalf of sinners. He was enduring the very essence of hell itself for us. He took our sin upon himself, and the holy God turned away from his beloved Son. William Hendriksen puts it in these memorable words: 'Hell came to Calvary that day, and the Saviour descended into it and bore its horrors in our stead.'[4]

As far as the Christian is concerned, three statements perfectly capture what the cross of Jesus was all about: 'I deserve hell. Jesus took my hell. There is nothing left now for me except heaven.'

If thou has my discharge procured,
And freely in my room endured
The whole of wrath divine;
Payment God cannot twice demand
First at my bleeding Surety's hand,
And then again at mine.

(Augustus M. Toplady)

Two appeals

In the light of what Jesus did on the cross, I would make two appeals. First, I would appeal to all who have received his salvation to think anew on how much you owe him.

The physical aspects of the crucifixion are too horrific and terrible for words. The crown of thorns, the scourging, the nails in his hands and feet and the humiliation of it all are beyond our ability to describe. But the hardest part of the whole experience for Jesus was not the physical sufferings, terrible as they were. The worst part for Jesus was the period of time in which he was rejected by both heaven and earth, those hours in which he became sin for us and was separated from God.

Jesus had lived his whole life in communion with the Father, but on the cross he was separated from the Father. And the thing that continually amazes and astounds me is that he bore it all for undeserving sinners like you and me. Because Jesus cried, 'My God, my God, why have you forsaken me?' I will not have to cry it in eternity.

His body broken, nail'd, and torn,
And stain'd with streams of blood,
His spotless soul was left forlorn,

Forsaken of his God.
'Twas then his Father gave the stroke,
That justice did decree;
All nature felt the dreadful stroke,
When Jesus died for me.

'Eli lama sabachthani,
My God, my God,' he cried,
'Why hast thou thus forsaken me?'
And thus my Saviour died.
But why did God forsake his Son,
When bleeding on the tree?
He died for sins, but not his own,
For Jesus died for me.

My guilt was on my Surety laid
And therefore he must die;
His soul a sacrifice was made
For such a worm as I.
Was ever love so great as this?
Was ever grace so free?
This is my glory, joy and bliss,
That Jesus died for me.

                                        (Author unknown)

Yes, I am amazed, as I reflect upon the penalty he endured,
that he could love me, a guilty sinner, so much, and I am also
amazed that I do not love him more and serve him better.

I would also appeal to all who have not yet received the
salvation provided by the Lord Jesus Christ. I urge you to think
deeply and seriously about what awaits those apart from
Christ. Look at the cross for a small glimmer of what hell is
like. Look at the garden of Gethsemane for another small
glimmer. There the Lord Jesus, as we saw in an earlier chapter,

contemplated drinking the cup of God's wrath on the cross and shrank from it. Mark describes that experience by saying Jesus was 'sore amazed' in the garden (Mark 14:33, AV). A. W. Pink says this signifies 'the greatest extremity of amazement, such as makes one's hair stand on end and ... flesh to creep'.[5] Mark goes on to say that there in Gethsemane Jesus began to be 'very heavy'. Pink says this means 'an utter sinking of spirit' and he suggests that the thought of enduring the wrath of God melted the heart of Jesus 'like wax'.[6]

If the thought of enduring the wrath of God had such a profound effect on the Lord Jesus, how much more effect should it have upon all those whose feet are hastening towards the wrath of God?

The good news is that we do not have to experience God's wrath. The Lord Jesus Christ has paid the penalty in full for all those who turn from their sins and receive him as their Lord and Saviour. All who do so gladly join Elvina M. Hall in these words:

> Jesus paid it all,
> All to him I owe;
> Sin had left a crimson stain,
> He washed it white as snow.

25.
Christ showing his credentials

John 19:28-30

We have no trouble seeing the spiritual value of the first four sayings of Jesus from the cross. A moment's meditation on each of them is all that is necessary to set our minds and hearts racing. But one glance at the words 'I thirst', and we are tempted to move quickly on. There does not seem to be much value in them. We err if we leap to such a conclusion. These words and the context in which John sets them actually embody exceedingly important and crucial truths.

The genuine humanity of Jesus

The first thing revealed by Jesus' cry, 'I thirst,' is the genuineness of his humanity. This is a crucial aspect of the plan of redemption that must be emphasized again and again. The nub of the matter is, to put it plainly, that there would be absolutely no salvation for anyone if the humanity of Christ was not real.

The reason for this is not hard to grasp. It was humanity that sinned against God, and God's justice demanded that humanity pay the penalty of sin. That penalty can either be paid by each individual sinner, or it can be paid by a substitute. Jesus Christ came to be the substitute. He came to endure the penalty due to his people. He had to be a man in order to do this.

Scripture also makes clear that, while he was truly man, he was more than man. He still retained his deity. Here we come to one of the central marvels of his redeeming work. Since he was a man he could suffer as a man, but since he was the God-man, he could also suffer for more than one man. Furthermore, he was able to suffer in a finite period of time an infinite amount of wrath.

The cry 'I thirst' is a human cry. It had been a period of several hours since a cup had last touched Jesus' lips. It probably was early the night before when he had supper with his disciples.

Think of all he had been through from that time. He had spent several hours praying in deepest agony of soul in the Garden of Gethsemane. While there he was taken into custody. He was manœuvred through various 'legal' proceedings. Then he was handed over to the Roman soldiers who proceeded to scourge him, crown him with thorns and mock him.

By the time Jesus spoke these words, he had been on the cross for a period of six hours. Herschel Ford says crucifixion is 'the most painful mode of torture ever conceived by man', and points out that the steady loss of blood brings on 'intensive thirst'.[1]

Bruce Milne, in his commentary on John's Gospel, also mentions 'the dehydration which was a prominent feature in the torture of crucifixion', and, in the light of it, says the cry of Jesus was 'wholly comprehensible'.[2]

How thankful we should be for this cry! The other sayings of Jesus from the cross are of such a nature that we might be inclined to think Christ's humanity was not real, that he was God in an imitation humanity and, therefore, did not really feel any pain while he was on the cross. The cry 'I thirst' brings us back with a jolt from such imaginings. Jesus' thirst was real. Since it was real, his humanity was real. And since his humanity was real, he met this essential qualification for providing atonement.

We surely have to stand amazed at what he was willing to do for his people. He was not only willing to take our humanity but also to go so far in that humanity as to suffer burning thirst. Why did he do it? What possessed him to go to such lengths? Why would he cross that enormous chasm between heaven's glory and the extreme agony of excruciating thirst on a Roman cross? He did it all for his people. He endured physical thirst so that they will never have to endure spiritual thirst. In his humanity he thirsted for water so that we shall never have to thirst for God.

> I heard the voice of Jesus say,
> 'Behold, I freely give
> The living water; thirsty one,
> Stoop down and drink, and live.'
> I came to Jesus, and I drank
> Of that life-giving stream;
> My thirst was quenched, my soul revived,
> And now I live in him.
>
> (Horatius Bonar)

We can explain Jesus' willingness to stoop so low in another way. We can say he was willing to thirst on the cross because of another thirst that burned inside him, the thirst for the souls of his people. Cecil Frances Alexander captures this thought in these lines:

> His are the thousand sparkling rills
> That from a thousand fountains burst,
> And fill with music all the hills;
> And yet he saith, 'I thirst.'

But more than pains that racked him then
Was the deep longing thirst divine
That thirsted for the souls of men;
Dear Lord, and one was mine!

The fulfilment of prophecy

That brings us to another aspect of the thirst of Christ, namely, the context in which John places these words. He writes, 'After this, Jesus, knowing that all things were now accomplished, that the Scriptures might be fulfilled, said, "I thirst!"'

The impression we get from these words is of Jesus keeping a mental checklist. He had already suffered the wrath of God on behalf of sinners, but one more thing remained. The redemption that he was providing by his death had been anticipated in the Old Testament in striking detail. Included in those prophecies was the promise that he would be given vinegar to drink (Ps. 69:21).

In order to prompt this fulfilment Jesus cried, 'I thirst!' The cry had its desired effect. The vinegar was immediately offered, and Jesus drank of it. It is no accident that John writes, 'So when Jesus had received the sour wine, he said, "It is finished!"' (John 19:30).

We are mistaken if we think of Jesus on the cross as nothing more than a poor, passive victim. He was far more than that. He actively worked at his death to make sure it was exactly what the Father had promised it would be. It is tempting to think of Christ as a conductor and the various details of his crucifixion as the instruments of an orchestra. Under his conductorship, all the details were brought into harmony without so much as a single discordant note.

By emphasizing the fulfilment of prophecy, John gives us another proof of the validity of Jesus' claims. This was, of course, one of John's main concerns, and in his Gospel he labours diligently to prove that Jesus really was who he claimed to be. He points to seven signs that Jesus performed, signs that were extremely well attested because they were performed in the midst of many witnesses. But as powerful and convincing as the signs and witnesses to Jesus are, there is probably no greater proof for the validity of his claims than fulfilled prophecy. It is, of course, one thing to know that Jesus fulfilled prophecy. It is another thing to realize the profound implications of this. Most know Jesus was supposed to have fulfilled the prophecies of the Old Testament, but very few seem to have any understanding of just how overwhelming this evidence is.

Josh McDowell helps us at this point. In his book *Evidence that Demands a Verdict*, he tabulates sixty-one major prophecies that Jesus fulfilled in his life and death. Amazingly enough, Jesus fulfilled twenty-nine of these on the last day of his life. These prophecies were made by different men during the five centuries from 1000 to 500 B.C.[3]

McDowell shows us the profound meaning of fulfilled prophecy by citing Peter Stoner's book, *Science Speaks*. In it Stoner calculates the probability of one man fulfilling forty-eight of these prophecies. It would be equal to a blindfolded man selecting a specially marked electron from an inch of electrons. How many electrons are there in an inch? If we counted 250 each minute, and if we counted day and night, it would take us nineteen million years to count the electrons in a one-inch line of electrons! What chance would a man have of selecting a single, marked electron among so many? The same as one man had of fulfilling forty-eight prophecies of the Old Testament! And Jesus fulfilled at least sixty-one![4]

Ours is a day in which people speak of truth as something that is always fluctuating and changing. It is seen as a different thing for different people and it even becomes different for each individual as his circumstances and surroundings change. Take the time to survey the prophecies Jesus fulfilled and you will soon see that Jesus is not just true for some people under some circumstances, but he is true for all people under all circumstances. The fact that he so minutely fulfilled so many prophecies forces upon us a couple of indisputable conclusions. One is that he is exactly what the Bible proclaims him to be — the eternal Son of God. If he is the Son of God, we are led inexorably to the next conclusion: what he says is true and must be obeyed.

26.
Christ finishing the task

John 19:30

It is not too much to say that from the moment the Father, the Son and the Holy Spirit agreed upon the plan of redemption they began to look forward to one word being spoken. That word, *'tetelestai,'* is translated with three words in English: 'It is finished.'

That single word would finally signal the completion of their plan. When it was at last uttered it indicated that nothing remained to be done concerning the provision of salvation. The redemption of souls from eternal destruction has to be considered the most important matter in all of human history. Therefore, the word that signalled the accomplishment of that redemption has to be considered the most significant word ever spoken.

All the promises and types of the Old Testament looked forward to that word. Jesus left heaven and took our humanity for the sole purpose of uttering that word. Yes, his coming can be reduced to that single word! All that he did during his earthly life and ministry was in preparation for that one word. He endured the intense agony of Gethsemane and the anguish of the cross so that he could utter that one word.

Six long hours he has been on the cross. Every prophecy has been fulfilled; not one is missing. The wrath of God has been endured in fullest measure. The cup is now empty. And Jesus cries, 'It is finished!' All of heaven has been focused on that cry, and it is now uttered. Heaven cheers. Hell trembles.

Jonathan Edwards says of Christ's cry:

> And thus was finished the greatest and most wonderful thing that was ever done. Now the angels beheld the most wonderful sight that ever they saw. Now was accomplished the main thing that had been pointed at by the various institutions of the ceremonial law, by all the typical dispensations, and by all the sacrifices from the beginning of the world...
>
> Then was finished that great work, the purchase of our redemption, for which such great preparation had been made from the beginning of the world. Then was finished all that was required in order to satisfy the threatenings of the law, and all that was necessary in order to satisfy divine justice; then the utmost that vindictive justice demanded, even the whole debt, was paid. Then was finished the whole of the purchase of eternal life. And now there is no need of anything more to be done towards a purchase of salvation for sinners; nor has ever anything been done since, nor will anything more be done for ever and ever.[1]

We must not slight this word. We must roll it over in our minds. Eternities are compressed here. Salvation rests here. This word requires us to go over ground we have been over before. It is ground we cannot traverse too often. This ground consists of what Jesus finished and how he finished it.

The great 'it' — what Jesus accomplished

We might be inclined to conclude that Jesus spoke this word out of relief that his agony was ending. Crucifixion was such an incredibly horrid and gruesome way to die that we can well imagine the victim gasping, 'It's over,' just before finally dying.

But when the Lord Jesus Christ said, 'It is finished!' he was not speaking as a tortured man who was glad to see suffering come to an end. These are not the last words of a poor, helpless victim who is happy to see the curtain of death drop. Although he suffered unplumbed depths of anguish and pain, this is not a last tortured gasp. It is not the final expression of agony.

There is all the difference in the world between finishing something and accomplishing something. When Jesus died he not only finished something; he accomplished something. What did he accomplish? We have a remarkable summary of it in Jesus' prayer in John 17. The opening words of that prayer take us to a time 'before the world was' (v. 5) and to three gifts the Father gave the Son. The first mentioned by the Lord is the gift of authority over all flesh (v. 2). The second is that gift that has occupied us so much in these pages, that is, the gift of a people to the Son by the Father. In this prayer the Lord Jesus specifically refers to this gift a total of seven times in six verses (vv. 2, 6, 9, 11, 12, 24).

The third gift was a work. Jesus says to the Father, 'I have finished the work which you have given me to do' (v. 4). Those words, spoken the night before he was crucified, are heavy with meaning. The work of the cross was so certain and definite that Jesus could speak of it in advance as already finished.

It is essential for us to understand that the one gift, the people, necessitated the other, the work. To receive the people, the Son would have to perform the work. The work, as we have noted time after time, was the work of redemption, or the work of the cross. The people whom the Father was giving to the Son would have to be redeemed from their sins, and that redemption could take place only through the Son's becoming their substitute and bearing in their place the punishment for their sin.

So when Jesus cried, 'It is finished!' he was referring both to the people and to the work the Father had given him. The 'it' comprehended and represented both. It was the work of dying on the cross to provide redemption for those whom the Father had given him. This 'it' to which Jesus referred is the theme which we have been tracing all along. It is the plan of salvation that was adopted by the triune God before the foundation of the world. It is the plan which was announced and pictured in the Garden of Eden and which was anticipated in promises and types throughout the entire Old Testament. It is the object which Jesus had in view when he left heaven to become God incarnate, when he stood with John the Baptist in the water of the Jordan and which he kept steadily in view as he conducted his public ministry. It is the goal which he unrelentingly approached even in the last hours of his life. It is the glorious plan of redemption.

Now we can see why these words ought to cause us to have a sense of awe. The salvation of sinners is not the haphazard work of a distraught God who frantically tries one thing and then another. It is rather the result of the triune God carrying out with perfect faithfulness a plan that stretches all the way back to that time when there was not even a world. What a tremendous truth is conveyed in this one little word 'it'! How it staggers and boggles our minds!

So when Jesus spoke these words on the cross, 'It is finished!', he was referring to that same 'it' — the salvation he and the Father had planned before the world was created. And in saying these words, he was not just giving up his last breath; he was speaking as a mighty victor who was crossing the finishing-line.

The finishing — how Jesus accomplished his mission

But let's now turn our attention away from the 'it' to the finishing, or to the accomplishing, of the task. Here we must deal with the question of what Jesus did to provide salvation. What he accomplished was the work of the cross to redeem the people the Father had given the Son. But what was necessary for Jesus to perform this redeeming work on the cross?

First, he had to come into this world as a man. He had to come to this world because it was the arena or realm in which the first Adam had failed. But he could not just come to this world as God. He had to come as man. He could not be the representative head of his people if he were not a man himself. This does not, of course, mean that he ceased to be God. God cannot stop being God. It means rather that he added to his deity our humanity so that he was at one and the same time fully God and fully man without any contradiction or confusion between the two.

As marvellous and glorious as his coming was, it was not sufficient in and of itself to save us. The Lord Jesus had yet more to do in order to accomplish redemption. For one thing, he had to live a life of sinlessness, a life of perfect obedience to the holy law of God. Why was this necessary? This was the requirement of God from the very beginning. If Adam and Eve had perfectly obeyed the one commandment God gave them in the garden of Eden they would have been given the gift of eternal life.

The one thing most people fail to realize about God's dealings with man is that God has never changed the condition for eternal life. Eternal life is only given to those who perfectly obey God, those who are perfectly righteous and without moral blemish. But Adam and Eve had not obeyed. They were not righteous. And all of us who have followed them are likewise disobedient and sinful.

The Lord Jesus Christ lived the sinless life that God demands. He did not fail at one single point. He did nothing wrong. He thought nothing wrong. He said nothing wrong. The Bible calls him 'a lamb without blemish and without spot' (1 Peter 1:19).

It was not enough for Jesus, however, to come and live a sinless life for us. We were already guilty of sin when he came. Something had to be done to pay for that sin. Here we come to the work of the cross. There the Lord Jesus Christ paid for our sins. He bore in his own body the penalty that was rightfully ours (1 Peter 2:24). There he endured the wrath of God on behalf of those whom the Father had given him.

By his life, then, the Lord Jesus provided the righteousness God demands of me to get into heaven. By his death, he paid for the sins that I have committed against God. When, by the grace of God, I came to Christ several years ago in repentance of my sins and in faith in him, my sins were counted as though they were Christ's and God declared them paid for, and Christ's righteousness was counted as though it were mine (2 Cor. 5:21). He took my sin; I receive his righteousness. My sin is paid for, and God's demand for righteousness is met. When Jesus cried, 'It is finished!' he was simply saying that he had done all that is necessary for believers to be saved.

Perhaps someone will ask about the resurrection. Is it not an essential part of the plan of salvation? It is indeed. Why then did Jesus say everything was finished before the resurrection? The answer is that he had done all that he came to do. It was the Father's work to raise him from the dead, and this the Father did (Acts 2:32; 17:31).

What should our response be to all of this? Those of us who are saved should break out in song and sound the trumpets of jubilee. We should daily praise God for such a glorious plan of salvation, and we should seek each day to bring honour and glory to his name.

Those who have not yet received the salvation provided by the life and death of Christ should flee to him at once. The work is done. There is nothing left to do except to bow by God's grace before the finished work of Christ and receive it.

Section III
From the cross

The cross of Christ is the focal point of human history. When it was raised against the sky, it split history into two halves. All of history prior to Jesus' death on Calvary can be seen in terms of his relentless approach to that cross. All of history subsequent to his death there must be seen in terms of his satisfied departure from it. But his satisfaction in his work on the cross was inseparably linked to his Father's being satisfied with the cross.

And all of that brings us to another dimension. Because God the Father and God the Son are satisfied with the cross, all those who believe are also satisfied with it.

27.
The Father satisfied

Matt. 27: 51; Acts 2:24,32-36

God the Father, God the Son and God the Holy Spirit entered into covenant with each other before the world began. There the Father gave the Son a people with the understanding that the Son would make atonement for their sins and thereby propitiate the Father's wrath against them. There the cross of Calvary was erected. There the Son of God agreed to become man and to go to that cross to make the atonement. From that time he began steadily and determinedly to approach that cross.

All through the long centuries of prophecy, at his baptism, in the wilderness, throughout his public ministry, even there in the anguish of Gethsemane, Jesus approached the cross.

Finally, the nails were hammered into his hands and feet. That long-expected cross was hoisted into the air. He hung suspended between heaven and earth. That point to which all history had moved was at last realized. The blood poured down. The sun hid its face. And he died. In keeping with the eternal covenant, Jesus Christ died on Calvary's cross.

That cross, as we have already noted, was necessary to satisfy the wrath of God. Did it achieve its purpose? Or did Christ die in vain? Was God the Father satisfied with what his Son did there on the cross? How do we know he was satisfied with his Son's death there? The Bible gives us the answer by emphatically pointing to four signal events.

The tearing of the veil

The first of these events was far more astonishing than most of us realize. It was the tearing of the thick, heavy curtain that separated the temple's Most Holy Place from the Holy of Holies. The Most Holy Place was the place where the high priest alone could enter once each year to make atonement for the sins of the people. William Hendriksen says of the curtain that sealed off the Most Holy Place: 'This inner curtain is the one described in Exod. 26:31-33; 36:35; II Chron. 3:14. As pictured in these passages, strands of blue, purple, and scarlet were interwoven into a white linen fabric, in such a manner that these colours formed a mass of cherubim, the guardian angels of God's holiness, symbolically as it were barring the way...'[1]

That curtain gave mute and eloquent testimony to a very solemn reality — namely, that man cannot stand before a holy God except on the basis of atonement for his sins. Even the atonement made by the High Priest once a year was not a sufficient basis for that curtain to be removed. The blood of animals could only anticipate the needed atonement; it certainly could not supply it.

Now it is three o'clock in the afternoon. The priests are busy at work in the temple. Caiaphas himself — he who had unwittingly prophesied that one must die for the whole nation so that the nation should not perish (John 11:50) — is busy in the temple. On Golgotha's hill outside the city the one whom Caiaphas and the religious leaders were so anxious to be rid of, Jesus, cries with a loud voice: 'Father, into your hands I commend my spirit' (Luke 23:46) and dies.

At that precise moment, that thickly-woven veil is torn from top to bottom as easily as a man would tear a sheet of paper in two. But this is not the hand of man; it is the hand of God! Imagine the astonishment of Caiaphas and all those in the temple as they hear the sound of that rending and then see the Most Holy Place standing naked before their eyes.

What did it mean? Why did God do this? It was his testimony, in the words of F. W. Krummacher, 'that the Levitical service, though divinely ordered and prophetically significant, contained only types of a coming salvation, which, now that the latter was accomplished, were rendered void, even as the blossom is expelled by the fruit'.[2]

In addition, it signified that sinners now have full and free access to God on the basis of Christ's death on the cross. Full atonement has been made. We can enter into the presence of God knowing Jesus Christ has fully satisfied the demands of his holy justice against us. Krummacher observes that Christ's act of mediation 'answered and fulfilled everything requisite for our justification in the sight of God, and, therefore, also for our admission before the throne of God'.[3]

That veil would not have been torn had God the Father not been completely and fully satisfied with his Son's atoning death.

The resurrection of Jesus

The second event through which God signalled his satisfaction with Christ's death was the resurrection. The consistent testimony of Scripture is that it was God the Father who raised Jesus from the dead, and that act evidenced his full approval of his Son (Acts 2:24,32; 4:10; 17:31).

The direction of the plan of redemption for the Lord Jesus Christ was down, down, down. He left the throne of heaven's glory to come down to this world of sin and darkness. How low he stooped! He traversed the massive gap between a throne in heaven and Bethlehem's stable and the carpenter's shop in Nazareth.

Perhaps the angels, as they witnessed it, said, 'He surely can't go any farther down than that.' But he did. He went down into the baptismal waters to freely identify himself with sinners.

Maybe when the angels saw that they said, 'That's as far down as he can go.' But he went further yet into the crucible of hostility during his public ministry. When the angels witnessed that, they may have remarked that he was down as far he could go. But as we follow him further, we find him in the depths of sorrow and anguish there in Gethsemane. And once again the angels must have wondered if it were possible for him to go any further.

The next day he went there to Golgotha to be crucified, and I can imagine the angels saying to each other, 'He has finally reached the bottom. He can surely go no further.' But as I look now at that cross, I see ladders being placed on each side of it, nails being removed, the limp, lifeless body of the Son of God slumping over a sturdy shoulder and being gently lowered to the ground. I see it now carried aside, washed and wrapped in linen cloths with spices being sprinkled in with each wrap. I see it gently carried to the tomb of Joseph of Arimathea. I see there in the gathering gloom strong shoulders being put to the massive rock in front of the tomb. I hear the grunts and the thud as that stone falls heavily into its place. And I hear the Father say to the angels of heaven, 'There! He has gone down as far as he can go!'

Yes, Jesus went all the way down into the very depths of death. But the glorious news of Scripture is that he didn't stay down.

Up from the grave he arose,
With a mighty triumph o'er his foes;
He arose a victor from the dark domain,

And he lives for ever with his saints to reign.
He arose! He arose! Hallelujah! Christ arose!

(Robert Lowery)

There can be no doubt about the significance of his resurrection. The apostle Paul says that through it Jesus was 'declared to be the Son of God with power' (Rom. 1:4). The Greek word that is translated 'declared' was originally used to describe the marking off of a field. It referred to something being clearly defined. What has been clearly defined by the resurrection of Jesus? What does it tell us about him? Paul tells us. It means he was no ordinary man, but was, in fact, exactly what he claimed to be — the Son of God.

But the apostle is not content merely to affirm that. He adds those two words, 'with power'. What is the significance of this? When the Son of God came into this world, he did not come as the Son of God with power. Far from it! He came as a helpless baby.

He was, of course, the Son of God even while he was that helpless infant in Bethlehem's manger. Make no mistake about that. Jesus Christ, the Second Person of the Trinity, was always God, and he did not give up his deity when he came to this world. But that deity, while still there, was veiled while he was here on earth.

Charles Wesley's unforgettable lines put it so well:

Veiled in flesh the Godhead see,
Hail th' incarnate Deity!

But when the Lord Jesus Christ arose from the grave, the veil was laid aside, and he was clearly shown to be what he had been all along — God in human flesh! He who had been 'made' flesh was 'declared' by the resurrection to be the Son of God. Mark Paul's words: the Son of God had to be 'made' flesh, but he did not have to be 'made' the Son of God. He was already that! All that was necessary was for him to be 'declared' to be the Son!

Who did this declaring? It was God the Father! And through this mighty declaration, God was pronouncing his verdict upon Jesus.

The wicked men who crucified Jesus had pronounced their verdict upon him. That cruel act was their way of saying Jesus was not God in human flesh, in other words, that he was an impostor. But their verdict was not God's. God, we might say, overturned their verdict and rendered it null and void by raising Jesus from the dead.

Each of us has also to render a verdict upon Jesus. We must either agree with those who crucified him, or with God the Father who raised him.

But there is even more to the resurrection of Jesus. The apostle Paul also tells us that we have 'justification' through that resurrection (Rom. 4:25). That word takes us to the very heart and soul of the Christian faith. It takes us into a courtroom. The judge in this courtroom in none other than the Judge of the whole world — God himself.

The Judge is also the supreme Law-giver. He has promulgated certain laws, and he has told us that we must live in obedience to those laws. He is perfect and holy himself, and he demands that each and every one of us bring a perfect holiness into his courtroom before he will allow us to enter into heaven. This puts us in a terrible dilemma because we have no righteousness to present to this Judge. All we have is sin.

All looks to be utterly hopeless but, thank God, there is hope. God, the perfect Law-giver and Judge, is also gracious. He takes no delight in the condemnation of sinners. So he himself has made a way for us to be forgiven and for us to have the righteousness he demands. That way is through his Son, Jesus Christ.

But what does all this have to do with the resurrection of Jesus? Why does Paul link our ability to stand before God, to present to him the righteousness he demands, with the resurrection of Jesus? Was it not the death of Christ on the cross by which atonement was made for sin? William Hendriksen provides the answer in these words: 'The Father, by raising Jesus from the dead, assures us that the atoning sacrifice has been accepted; hence, our sins are forgiven.'[4]

Martyn Lloyd-Jones explains it in this way: 'The resurrection is the proclamation of the fact that God is fully and completely satisfied with the work that his Son did upon the Cross... If God had not raised Him from the grave we might draw the conclusion that our Lord was not able to bear the punishment of the guilt of our sins, that it was too much for Him, and that His death was the end.'[5]

So we can say God made two declarations by raising Jesus from the dead. First, he declared him to be his Son. Secondly, he declared his work to be completely satisfactory.

The ascension of Jesus

After he arose from the grave, the Lord Jesus spent forty days with his disciples. During this time he furnished them with 'many infallible proofs' of his resurrection (Acts 1:3). When this period was over, he ascended to the Father in heaven (Acts 1:9).

The ascension does not seem to receive much attention or emphasis these days, but it is yet another of the vital links in the chain of redemption. It is one more way that the Father indicated his complete satisfaction with his Son and his work of redemption.

The Scriptures make it clear that Jesus was received in heaven by the Father. He was given a seat at the right hand of God (Eph. 1:20; Col. 3:1; Heb. 12:2). That is 'the seat of cosmic authority',[6] and he is even now reigning as king. Some place Christ's reign completely in the future, but on the Day of Pentecost the apostle Peter stood before the thousands gathered in Jerusalem to proclaim that Jesus began to reign as soon as he was seated at the Father's right hand. For proof of his assertion, Peter cited the coming of the Holy Spirit (Acts 2:33). The Holy Spirit is, then, the gift of the risen, reigning Christ to his followers to enable them to carry out his work in the world.

From that seat of authority, Jesus Christ also continues his work as our great High Priest. He intercedes for all those who come to God by him (Heb. 7:25), and he sympathizingly cares for the needs of his people (Heb. 4:14-16).

> He took his meritorious blood,
> And rose above the skies,
> And in the presence of his God,
> Presents his sacrifice.
> His intercession must prevail,
> With such a glorious plea
> My cause can never, never fail,
> For Jesus died for me.
>
>   (Author unknown)

We should note yet another implication of the ascension — one that very few seem to ponder. When Jesus ascended to the Father, he took our humanity back into glory with him. Here again we see the marvel of his grace. When he took on himself our humanity, he did not do so just for the years he was here on earth, but for ever. The Lord Jesus did not cease to be a man after he went back into heaven. He now has a glorified body, but it is still a body — the same type of body believers will receive when he finally returns from heaven to take them unto himself.

The sending of the Holy Spirit

A further sign of the Father's satisfaction with his Son's atoning death is found fifty days after Jesus arose from the grave. Before he was crucified, Jesus spoke these words to his disciples: 'And I will pray the Father, and he will give you another Helper, that he may abide with you for ever, even the Spirit of truth, whom the world cannot receive, because it neither sees him nor knows him; but you know him, for he dwells with you and will be in you' (John 14:16).

That promise was fulfilled on the Day of Pentecost. As the disciples were waiting in Jerusalem for this promise to be fulfilled, 'There came a sound from heaven, as of a rushing mighty wind, and it filled the whole house where they were sitting' (Acts 2:2).

The coming of the Holy Spirit was indisputable proof that the Father had heard and answered the prayer Jesus had promised to pray. We may be sure the Father would not have heard this prayer, and the Spirit would not have been sent, if the Father had not been completely satisfied with his Son's death on the cross.

The rending of the veil, the resurrection, the ascension and the coming of the Holy Spirit merge their individual voices into a single, mighty, indisputable testimony that the God before whom we must eventually stand and give account has been completely satisfied by the work of his Son. Because of that, all who belong to him can stand on that awesome day without fear.

28.
Jesus satisfied

Hebrews 12:2

What caused Jesus to go to the cross? His fidelity to the Father's will? Emphatically yes. His love for sinners? Yes. But also his inexpressible, abounding joy. Can we really speak of joy for Christ in the cross? Yes. The author of Hebrews says that Jesus '... for the joy that was set before him endured the cross' (Heb. 12:2).

We know there is joy in the cross for us. Through that cross we have forgiveness for our sins, deliverance from eternal condemnation and acceptance before God. But where was the joy in the cross for Jesus?

The joy of redeeming the love-gift

Remember that the Son of God was given a love-gift by the Father before the world began. That love-gift consisted of a people. But before that people could become the Son's, they had to be redeemed from their sin. The penalty for their sin had to be paid for by the Son. The Son's death on the cross was the means by which they were to be redeemed. The joy of the cross for Jesus was, then, in paying for the sins of these people so they could become his.

We should not, therefore, look at the Son as coming reluctantly to perform the work of redemption. His was no shuffling, grudging obedience. It was a glad, eager, ready obedience.

Yes, that cross meant untold suffering and anguish. Yes, he endured incredible hostility and hardship as he journeyed through his public ministry to that cross. Yes, he knew humiliating shame. And yet there was a sense in which — if we may reverently put it like this — the Lord Jesus Christ could hardly wait to get to that cross because of the joy of making atonement for that love-gift. The joy was worth the pain.

On the night before he was crucified, the Lord Jesus saw the pain and the sorrow etched on the faces of the disciples. He had told them he was about to leave them, and they were crushed. He softened the blow for them with these words: 'Most assuredly, I say to you that you will weep and lament, but the world will rejoice; and you will be sorrowful, but your sorrow will be turned into joy. A woman, when she is in labour, has sorrow because her hour has come; but as soon as she has given birth to the child, she no longer remembers the anguish, for joy that a human being has been born into the world' (John 16:20-21).

What Jesus said that night to his disciples, he could equally well have said of himself. He knew all about the sorrow and anguish of the cross, but for him, as for the mother bearing a child, the joy of the result made it all worthwhile.

The joy of receiving the love-gift as his bride

Few of life's events bring more happiness and joy than weddings. Two people, deeply in love, commit themselves to each other for the rest of their lives.

Scripture uses the joy of a wedding to convey Christ's relationship to the church. In his discussion of the relationship of husbands and wives, the apostle Paul refers to Christ's love for the church (Eph. 5:22-33). Clearly, he intends us to understand that the church is the bride of Christ.

The apostle John carries the theme even further in describing his vision of a coming day: 'And I heard, as it were, the voice of a great multitude, as the sound of many waters and as the sound of mighty thunders saying, "Alleluia! For the Lord God Omnipotent reigns! Let us be glad and rejoice and give him glory, for the marriage of the Lamb has come and his wife has made herself ready"' (Rev. 19:6-7).

The fullest glimpse into the marriage of Christ to his church comes, suprisingly enough, not from the New Testament but from Psalm 45. The author of that psalm had evidently been commissioned to write about the marriage of the king of his nation. As he considered that event, remarkable enough in its own way, he was enabled to write prophetically about a far more magnificent wedding — namely, the wedding of the Messiah and his bride, the church.

The wedding day of those times proceeded along these general lines. The bride and her attendants would gather in the home of the bride's father where they would put on their finest clothes. Meanwhile the groom and his attendants would gather at his home to do the same. When the bridegroom's party were ready they would proceed through the streets of the city to the bride's home and would escort her and her entourage back to his home. A joyful wedding feast would ensue, lasting for a period of several days.

This pattern is evident in the psalm. Verses 2-9 tell us about the bride waiting for her groom. In particular they relate to us some of what goes through her mind at this time. Verses 10-12 tell us how the bride is comforted and reassured while she waits. The psalm comes to a joyous climax with verses 13-15 as the groom finally arrives and the bride is presented to him. The bride's attendants come out to greet him and to assure him that the bride is ready, that she has attired herself in clothing 'woven with gold' (v. 13), and that she will soon be presented to him in 'robes of many colours' (v. 14). That moment of meeting is followed by the procession back to the groom's palace (for he is the king) and to the marriage feast.

All of this, by the inspiration of the Holy Spirit, is designed to make us think about that unspeakably grand moment when the Lord Jesus will return to claim his bride. When he comes he will find her arrayed in the garment that he himself provided for her — the garment of perfect righteousness. He will also find that she has been prepared by the sanctifying work of the Holy Spirit so that in addition to the outer garment of perfect righteousness she has an inner beauty about her.

God's plan of salvation finally culminates in those whom he gave to his Son in eternity past going back to the palace with him as his holy bride — back to the palace from which the Lord first came to redeem her unto himself, back past all the enemies that he defeated in order to save her. Yes, thank God, it will some day be 'back to the palace' for all those who know the Lord Jesus and make up his bride.

In his wonderful commentary on Psalm 45, Walter Chantry captures something of the significance of this day for those who refused Christ: 'Defeated foes watch in helpless ruin. Observing is the sceptic who once sneered that there was no reality to the Church's trust in the unseen King. All who laughed at the faith of the bride will watch her pass by at the side of her Lord, taken by him to be his holy bride. All who preferred a fallen world system with its pleasures and riches will sit amidst the ruins and ashes of that temporary order now demolished. They will lift their shameful heads to see the Church in a gown interwoven with gold, all radiant in the presence of her loving Lord, about to enter his kingdom and hers. No doubt will remain in any soul of the wisdom of waiting for Messiah and the foolishness of having scorned his offers of mercy. But the Church will pass them by. At that moment those who are accursed will be accursed still. They will have forever to envy the Church and regret their tragic rejection of her society on earth.'[1]

The joy of Christ over receiving the redeemed as his bride naturally leads to yet another joy.

The joy of seeing the love-gift gathered round him

Why was there so much joy for Jesus in paying the penalty for those given him by the Father? It is tempting when we are reading a particularly intriguing book to turn to the last chapter to see how it all turns out. If we turn to the last chapter of the Bible for a glimpse of the future, we find this description of the heavenly city that will be the home of the redeemed: 'And there shall be no more curse, but the throne of God and of the Lamb shall be in it, and his servants shall serve him. They shall see his face, and his name shall be on their foreheads' (Rev. 22:3-4).

Here we have at least part of the joy the Lord Jesus felt in going to the cross. The atonement he made there is going to yield a vast multitude of redeemed people who will faithfully serve him for ever and ever and who will perfectly reflect his character (his name represents his person, and the forehead represents visibility. Hence, the person of Christ will be visible in his redeemed people).

There they are, rank upon rank of them — all of them lost in wonder, love and praise; all of them freed from every last vestige of sin; all of them with bodies 'conformed to his glorious body' (Phil. 3:21); all of them ready to do his bidding. Death can no longer touch them. Their tears have been wiped away for ever. Pain and sorrow exist no more. And they are all there for one reason, and one reason only — the atoning death of Jesus Christ.

Isaiah 50:7 gives us some prophetic words that should be understood as nothing less than the words of the Lord Jesus Christ himself: 'Therefore I have set my face like a flint, and I know that I will not be ashamed.' As the Son of God looked in advance at his death on the cross, he knew he would not be ashamed or disappointed with what he would accomplish there. He knew in advance that he would be satisfied with his work there.

The 53rd chapter of Isaiah's prophecy gives us a fascinatingly detailed preview of the cross of Christ. Towards the end we read of Christ: 'He shall see his seed... He shall see the travail of his soul, and be satisfied' (Isa. 53:10-11). The 'seed' is the fruit, or the harvest, of Christ's atoning death. It consists of all those who come to faith in him. It is those whom the Father gave him before the foundation of the Lord.

It is surely correct to say that the Son of God saw them there in eternity past as he looked down the corridor of time. He must have seen them in his mind's eye as he was hanging there on the cross in agony and blood. He certainly sees them as they come to faith in him one by one. He obviously sees them as they come to the end of their earthly pilgrimage. He sends his angels to carry their souls into his presence, and he sees their bodies go into their graves.

Each of these 'seeings' must have been, or must be, deeply satisfying to our Lord. But there is no seeing like the last when redemption's work will finally be done and the love-gift will stand before him as the completed trophy of his redeeming death. He will see, and he will be satisfied.

Matthew Henry puts it admirably: 'The salvation of souls is a great satisfaction to the Lord Jesus. He will reckon all his pains well bestowed, and himself abundantly recompensed, if the many sons be by him brought through grace to glory. Let him have this, and he has enough. God will be glorified, penitent believers will be justified, and then Christ will be satisfied.'[2]

From Christ's satisfaction with his work of redemption, Henry proceeds to draw this conclusion: 'Thus, in conformity to Christ, it should be a satisfaction to us if we can do anything to serve the interests of God's kingdom in the world. Let it always be our meat and drink, as it was Christ's, to do God's will.'[3]

29.
The redeemed satisfied

Revelation 5:1-14

In Revelation chapter 5 we read of a most unusual choir — one that is made up of 'the four living creatures' (v. 8), 'the twenty-four elders' (v. 8), 'many angels' (v. 11) and 'every creature which is in heaven and on the earth and under the earth and such as are in the sea' (v. 13). That is quite a choir!

This choir sings 'a new song' (v. 9) which consists of three stanzas. The four living creatures and the twenty-four elders join together in singing the first stanza. They are joined in the second stanza by all the angels. And, finally, all of creation joins together in the third stanza. This is no small thing. Here we are confronted with a mighty, swelling anthem from an innumerable throng.

The four living creatures are of that high order of angels known as 'cherubim'. They have been previously described by the apostle John as being in strength like the lion, in ability to render service like the ox, in intelligence and purpose like man and in swiftness to serve like the eagle (Rev. 4:7).

The twenty-four elders represent the saints of all the ages. Combining the twelve patriarchs of the Old Testament with the twelve apostles of the New Testament gives us this representative number.

In John's vision, the saints joined with the four living creatures in singing these words:

You are worthy to take the scroll,
And to open its seals;
For you were slain,
And have redeemed us to God by your blood
Out of every tribe and tongue and people and nation,
And have made us kings and priests to our God;
And we shall reign on the earth

(vv. 9-10).

The source of their satisfaction — Jesus has taken the scroll

Notice how the saints refer to themselves in this refrain. They call themselves the 'redeemed' and 'kings and priests'. They have been plucked from the bondage of sin and elevated to the exalted level of serving as kings and priests. And, note it well, they ascribe all this to the Lord Jesus Christ and his atoning death on the cross. It is all through that cross that was erected back there in eternity past!

That redeeming work is presented in John's vision in terms of a scroll. Speculation has abounded about this scroll. There are several details about it that we should note.

First, *it is in the right hand of God*, which is always associated in Scripture with his power and authority. The scroll has to relate to authority, or to carry authority.

Secondly, *this scroll has writing on the inside and the reverse*. This indicates that it deals with a matter so huge that it requires all space available to deal with it.

Thirdly, this scroll is said to be *sealed with seven seals*. These seals are arranged so that when each is broken a portion of the scroll may be unrolled and read. When all the seals are broken, the entire scroll may be read.

Finally, we are told that *the scroll could only be opened and read by someone who was worthy to do so.* 'A strong angel' asks, 'Who is worthy to open the scroll and to loose its seals?' (v. 2). And, to John's deep dismay, 'No one in heaven or on the earth or under the earth' could be found even to look at the scroll, much less to open it and read it (vv. 3-4).

What is this scroll? It is the sum of God's decrees with respect to the universe. It is God's purpose for the universe. William Hendriksen says this scroll 'represents God's eternal Plan, his decree which is all-comprehensive'.[1] Hendriksen adds, 'It symbolizes God's purpose with respect to the *entire* universe *throughout* history, and concerning *all* creatures in *all* ages and unto all eternity'[2] (emphases are his).

If that scroll is not opened, God's purpose is not realized. But, thank God, there is one who has earned the right to open the book, to break the seals and to rule the universe according to God's plan. This one is none other than the Lord Jesus Christ. He is 'the Lion of the tribe of Judah, the Root of David' (v. 5). When he came to earth he came as a descendant of Judah and of David. He came as a lion, which means he came to conquer all the foes that would thwart the purpose of God.

Who are these foes? Satan and all his forces, sin and death — all may be considered enemies of God's purpose.

How is it that Christ was able to conquer these foes? It was, amazingly enough, by coming in the capacity of 'a Lamb' (v. 6).

The lamb is, of course, the animal of sacrifice. It was offered up in the place of the one who offered it. It was put to death in his place. Although innocent, it was put to death, taking the penalty that was due to the offerer.

Lambs could not, of course, actually take the place of human beings, but they could picture or represent one who could and did actually take the place of sinners. Jesus Christ is that perfect Lamb. In this vision, John saw him with seven horns and seven eyes (v. 6). The number seven represents perfection, while horns are to be associated with power and eyes with discernment. The fact, then, that Christ appeared with seven horns and seven eyes means he is perfect in power and perfect in discernment. His perfect discernment is due to the fact that he has 'seven Spirits', that is, that he is perfectly filled with the Holy Spirit.

In his capacity as the perfect Lamb, Jesus Christ did everything that was necessary to remove the obstacles to God's plan. There on the cross he defeated Satan, he paid for the sins of his people and removed the penalty of eternal death.

That cross down through the centuries has been an object of ridicule, scorn and shame. In our day the blood of Christ is dismissed as a repugnant thing. To be saved by blood! Such a thing is, as far as many are concerned, utterly disgusting and revolting. How unsophisticated and barbaric! This attitude has brought enormous pressure upon the people of God to be ashamed of the cross, to push it into the background in order to accommodate the intellectual sophistication of the age. And that pressure has always been there for the people of God.

But now at last, in the scene depicted in Revelation 5, the tides of time have broken on the shore of eternity, and the people of God enjoy the fruits of what that cross was all about. And, overwhelmed by it all, they break out into this song. This is the song of the satisfied! They look upon God the Father who planned, they look upon God the Son who executed, they look upon God the Spirit who applied, and the testimony of their united hearts is: 'He has done all things well.'

So God's purpose for the universe is realized through Christ's conquering, atoning death. And what is that purpose? We find it right here in the swelling anthem of this massive choir. God's purpose is to bring everything to this point of convergence — all creation joining together in acknowledgement that Jesus Christ is Lord of all.

There is nothing grander than God's plan of redemption. It is so grand and glorious that it will be the object of praise and worship in eternity. And eternity itself will not suffice to offer all the praise that is due to the Christ who purchased it.

Angels in shining order sit
Around my Saviour's throne;
They bow with reverence at his feet
And make his glories known.
Those happy spirits sing his praises
To all eternity;
But I can sing redeeming grace
For Jesus died for me.

Oh! Had I but an angel's voice
To bear my heart along,
My flowing numbers soon would raise
To an immortal song.
I'd charm their harps and golden lyres
In sweetest harmony,
And tell to all the heavenly choirs
That Jesus died for me.

(Author unknown)

Section IV
Responding to the journey

The drama of redemption stretches from eternity to eternity. It is vast and mind-boggling. I stand in awe and wonder. I was given by the Father to the Son before the world began! Amazing! The Son agreed to take my humanity and to die in shame and agony on the cross to purchase me. He began there in eternity past to move towards that cross. Steadily, with incredible love for the Father and for those given him by the Father, he approached that cross. He died there for those people. He died there for me. I am part of something that is stupendous and magnificent. I am caught up in the love relationship of the triune God. I am caught up in something that is eternal.

I cannot even begin to take all this in. The cross of Christ was not the result of an unfortunate, unforeseen turn of circumstances. It was all laid out ahead of time. It did not take God the Father or God the Son by surprise. They, in league with God the Spirit, planned Jesus' death on that cross and set the date for it to take place. When the hammers of the soldiers did their grim work, it was at the precise moment the triune God had set.

How do I respond to such stupendous, overwhelming truth? Truth such as this will not allow me to be lost in mere temporary, trivial concerns. I cannot stare truth like this in the face, and then just shrug and walk away. I cannot dismiss it by saying, 'That's nice,' and then go off to embrace meaningless trinkets and baubles. Such truth demands the response of faith and the response of love.

30.
The response of faith

Romans 3:21-31

Jesus' death on the cross was not an afterthought on God's part. It was the plan and purpose of God from the very beginning. It was anticipated in the books of Moses, in the Psalms and in the Prophets. The Lord Jesus asserted as much in his conversation with his disciples on the evening of the day of his resurrection (Luke 24:44).

As we have seen, the Old Testament anticipated the cross in two ways: through promises and types. Both are found in the garden of Eden. There God made the first promise of redemption (Gen. 3:15), and there God first gave a type, or picture, of it by slaying animals and clothing Adam and Eve with their skins (Gen. 3:21). From that beginning, we find a steady stream of both promises and types in the Old Testament, and that stream continued to roll along, ever deepening and widening in its flow, until it finally culminated in Christ's death on Calvary's cross.

Those promises and types clearly indicated that the death of Christ was to be no ordinary death, that through that death Christ would take the place of sinners and bear the penalty of God's wrath — the penalty they themselves so richly deserved. In taking their place and bearing God's wrath against them, Christ would free them from that wrath. God's justice only demands that sin be paid for once. If Christ pays for it there is no penalty left for the sinner to pay.

Paul picks up this stream of thought with that word 'propitiation'. That word means God's wrath against the sinner has been averted, or turned away. And, as we have noted, it can only be diverted from the sinner by a substitute coming between the sinner and God to receive, or absorb, it.

A matter of crucial importance

Now we come to a matter of crucial importance. We can put it in the form of this question: how does the death of Christ come to count for the individual?

Some are not troubled about this matter at all. As far as they are concerned, nothing is more needless and silly than to ask how the death of Christ is applied to the individual because, they argue, it already applies to every individual. One preacher of this persuasion went so far to put it like this: 'In the end everybody will be saved. I have hope even for the devil.'[1]

What shall we say to this argument? Does the Bible allow us to be universalists? Does it teach that the death of Christ automatically counts for all?

On page after page, the biblical authors plainly give the same answer. The saving work of Christ does *not* count for all, but for those whom the Father gave him before the world began. These are the ones whom the Holy Spirit regenerates and effectually draws to him. And these are the ones who by faith receive the finished work of Christ. In fact, this answer is so plain in Scripture that we finally have to say that those who fail to see it do so, not because it is not there, but rather because they do not want it to be there.

In the verses before us, the apostle Paul is exceedingly straightforward about the matter. He says the saving work of

Christ only applies to those who receive it by faith. Eight times in these verses he uses the word 'faith' (vv. 22,25,26,27,28, 30,31).

We should note that this emphasis comes hard on the heels of a section in which Paul hammers on the universality of sin. He writes:

> There is none righteous, no, not one;
> There is none who understands;
> There is none who seeks after God.
> They have all gone out of the way;
> They have together become unprofitable;
> There is none who does good, no, not one
>
> (Rom. 3:10-12).

The words 'none' and 'all' and the phrase 'no, not one' come in trip-hammer fashion and leave no room at all for manœuvre. All are 'under sin' (Rom. 3:9).

From the grim picture of universal sin, Paul proceeds to the happy news that God has provided salvation for sinners in and through his Son, Jesus Christ. But he does not now use the same universal language he used in describing man's sinful condition. His language is now strikingly particular. Salvation does not apply to 'all', but rather to 'all who believe' (v. 22). It is for 'the one who has faith in Jesus' (v. 26). The very nature of Christ's death, substitution for the sinner, defines its scope — those whom the Father gave him.

If Paul intended to teach a universal salvation, he would surely have done so in conjunction with his teaching on the universality of sin, but he did not do so. When dealing with sin, he stressed universality. When dealing with salvation, he stressed particularity. While the death of Christ is sufficient for all, it is efficient for the people given to Christ by the Father before the foundation of the world. And they receive the benefit of his death by faith. Paul emphatically says those who have this faith are the ones for whom the death of Christ avails. Those who do not have this faith are the ones for whom the death of Christ does not avail. In doing so, he is essentially repeating what the apostle John records in his Gospel: 'He who believes in the Son has everlasting life; and he who does not believe the Son shall not see life, but the wrath of God abides on him' (John 3:36).

Faith, then, is the means by which we receive the benefits secured by the Lord Jesus dying on the cross. It is urgent, therefore, for us to understand this matter of faith.

When we come to this subject, we must immediately be on guard against two kinds of dangers. One is to make faith less than it should be; the other is to make faith more than it should be.

Making faith less than it should be

Stopping short of true commitment

Let's look at how can we make faith less than it should be. Biblical faith consists of hearing the message of the gospel, believing that message to be true, and committing ourselves to that message.

We might say faith has an ear that enables it to hear the gospel. It also has a mind to consent to the truth of that message. And it has a hand actually to receive the message. We make faith less than biblical faith when we stop short of that final stage of actually committing ourselves to the gospel message.

In other words, we can have the knowledge of the gospel, that is, know what the gospel alleges and affirms. But that is not biblical faith. It is only intellectual apprehension of facts.

We can go even further and believe the gospel is true. We can hear what the Bible says about our sinful condition, about God's holiness and judgement to come and about God's plan of salvation in Christ. We can hear it all and nod in agreement. We can say, 'Yes, I know I'm a sinner who is bound for judgement. Yes, I know Christ is the Son of God, and that he, and he alone, is the Saviour. Yes, I know that on the cross he did everything necessary for my sins to be forgiven.'

We can say all this from the heart, firmly believing it is all true as we say it, and still not have true faith.

True faith carries us on to the next level, which is actually to commit ourselves to the truth of this message, to rest ourselves entirely upon it as the only hope for our salvation. Jim Elliff illustrates biblical faith in this way:

> Suppose that my watch had stopped running; so I asked you to give me the name of the best watch repairman in the city. You highly recommended one particular man whom you and others consider the expert in watch repair. I believe you and make the trip into the city to locate his shop.
>
> The shop is a quaint old place having been in operation for over fifty years. I find many certificates of commendation of the walls, all of which make me more of a believer. With watch still on my wrist, I press it up against the thick glass between the expert and me. I ask 'Can you fix this kind of watch?' Without hesitancy, the repairman replies, 'Why, certainly, I know everything about them and have all the parts in stock.'
>
> We stand there looking at each other awkwardly for a few unpleasant moments until the man asks me, 'Are you going to give me the watch?' 'No!' I blurt out. 'No sir, not at all. My father gave me this watch and I am not about to give it to you. I know what you "experts" do

with watches like this. You take out the insides and
replace them with inferior workmanship. No sir, you'll
not have my watch!'

The surprised watchman then makes a profound
observation: 'Well, if you don't give it to me, I can't fix
it.'[2]

To get a broken watch repaired, one has to give it in abandoned trust to the watch-repairer. In like manner the one who
wants to have his broken soul repaired must give it to Christ in
abandoned trust.

Divorcing faith from works

Another way in which many make faith less than it should be
is to suggest that it is possible to have it and not be concerned
about living for the Lord Jesus Christ. While it is faith alone
that saves, saving faith is never alone. It always leads to good
works. We cannot work for our salvation, but if we have been
saved we will certainly manifest it in good works.

John Flavel provides insight on this matter by anticipating
this objection: 'But if Christ wrought so hard, we may sit still.
If he finished the work, nothing remains for us to do.'

Flavel answers that objection in this way: 'Nothing of that
work which Christ did, remains for you to do. It is your
commendation and duty to leave all that to Christ: but there is
other work for you to do... You must work as well as Christ,
though not the same ends Christ did. He wrought hard to
satisfy the law, by fulfilling all righteousness. He wrought all
his life long, to work out a righteousness to justify you before
God. This work falls to no hand but Christ's: but you must
work, to obey the commands of Christ into whose right ye are
come by redemption: you must work to testify your thankful-
ness to Christ, for the work finished for you: you must work,

to glorify God by your obedience: *let your light so shine before men.* For these, and divers other such ends and reasons, your life must be a working life. God preserve all his people from the gross and vile opinions of *Antinomian libertines,* who cry up grace and decry obedience'[3] (italics are his).

Making faith more than it should be

The second danger we must guard against is to make faith more than it should be. We do this when we make faith a good work that we perform in order to secure salvation.

The whole purpose of God in salvation is not only to provide a way of forgiveness for sinners but to do so in a way that brings honour and glory to himself. Since God is perfection in every way, it is only right for him to seek glory for himself.

Now how does he glorify himself in this business of salvation? He does so by removing all grounds for any to boast. This is the reason salvation cannot be achieved by good works. If it could, there would indeed be something for us to boast about. We could talk about how we had lived such good lives that we earned heaven.

Paul makes this point very clear. He says God has devised salvation in such a way that boasting is 'excluded' (v. 27). There is no room for it at all. How is it excluded? Paul's answer is 'by the law of faith' (v. 27).

Faith by its very nature leaves no credit for us. It is not a work that we do to earn our salvation. If it were, there would be something for us to boast about. We would be able to say, 'We are saved because we had enough insight to believe and others did not.'

John R. W. Stott puts it in this way: 'It is vital to affirm that there is nothing meritorious about faith, and that, when we say that salvation is "by faith, not by works", we are not substituting one kind of merit ("faith") for another ("works").'[4]

Why is it that we can take no credit for our faith? One reason is that we do not produce it. It is given to us. The apostle Paul says, 'For by grace you have been saved through faith, and that not of yourselves; it is the gift of God, not of works, lest anyone should boast' (Eph. 2:8-9).

In his letter to the Philippians, Paul says their ability to believe in Christ had been 'granted' to them (Phil. 1:29). Faith is not something the people of God work up in themselves. It is produced by the Holy Spirit when he regenerates the unbeliever and draws him or her to Christ.

Another reason why we can take no credit for faith is that it is of such a nature that it will not allow us to do so. True faith does not look to itself. It looks to Christ, and to him alone, as the only hope of salvation. We are not saved by faith in faith, but rather by faith in Christ.

This is biblical faith. It looks away from itself and rests entirely on the finished work of the Lord Jesus Christ. If Christ finished the work of salvation, what can we do except receive it? A finished work demands faith plus nothing. Flavel again beautifully makes the point: 'If he have finished the work what need of our additions? And if not, to what purpose are they? Can we finish that which Christ himself could not? But we would fain be sharing with him in this honour, which he will never endure. Did he finish the work by himself, and will he ever divide the glory and praise of it with us? No, no, Christ is no half Saviour. Oh it is an hard thing to bring these proud hearts to live upon Christ for righteousness: we would fain add our penny to make up Christ's sum. But if you would have it so ... you and your penny must perish together.'[5]

31.
The response of love

John 12:1-8

Those who by God's grace have come to understand the cross of Christ and to rest in the redemption he provided there gladly join Isaac Watts in saying:

> Love so amazing, so divine
> Demands my soul, my life, my all.

The love of God in Christ calls for love from me — a fiery, burning love.

> Your love endured the cross, despising all the shame.
> That afternoon when midnight fell, your suff'ring
>   cleared my name.
> And that sin-swept hill became the open door to paradise
> Because you paid much too high a price...

> You deserve a fiery love that won't ignore your sacrifice
> Because you paid much too high a price.

> Your grace inspires my heart to rise above the sin
> And all the earthly vanity that seeks to draw me in.
> I want to tell a jaded world of love that truly saved my life,
> A love that paid so high a price.
>   (Phill McHugh)

There is no passage that so challenges me on this point of my love for Christ as John 12. There I find Mary bowing in wonder and adoration before Jesus to pour out costly ointment upon him. Her example forces me to examine myself and moves me to pour out the ointment of my life in adoring service to the Lord who loved me and gave himself for me.

The sight of Jesus sitting there at the table with the brother she thought she had lost overwhelmed Mary. On top of that, she realized that Jesus himself was about to die (v. 7). Jesus had predicted it on several occasions, but only Mary seems to have really understood what it was all about. William Hendriksen says, 'Mary was, perhaps, the best listener Jesus ever had.'[1]

She left the room for a moment, returned with some very costly ointment and anointed Jesus' head (Matt. 26:7) and his feet. She then, in violation of the customs of her day, loosed her long hair in public and began to dry Jesus' feet with her hair.

This passage has always seemed to me to be one of the most moving and powerful in all Scripture. It forces me to examine myself. I cannot read it without asking myself two pointed questions.

Do I love Christ?

First, I ask, do I love Christ? Perhaps someone will respond to that question by saying, 'Well, it's easy to see why Mary loved Jesus. After all, he did raise her brother from the dead. Anyone who experienced that would love Christ.'

We have just as many powerful and compelling reasons to love Christ as Mary did. The fact is that every Christian has already experienced something far more significant than Mary, Martha and Lazarus experienced. Each child of God has already had a resurrection of his or her own. The Bible tells us we were all 'dead in trespasses and sins' (Eph. 2:1), but God, through the work of the Lord Jesus Christ on the cross, has 'made us alive together with Christ' (Eph. 2:5) and 'raised us up together' (Eph. 2:6).

This is not just true of some Christians, but of all without exception. This has already happened to each child of God for the simple reason that one cannot be a child of God without it.

But there is another resurrection awaiting the child of God — the resurrection of the body. When a believer dies we take his body and place it in a grave, but the Bible makes it clear that the grave is not the final word for that body. A glad day is coming when the body of each believer is going to be raised from the dead. Jesus Christ himself is going to return to this earth with a blast from the heavenly trumpet and with the shout of the archangel, and all the 'dead in Christ' will rise from their graves (1 Thess. 4:16), and will receive new bodies like the glorious body the Lord Jesus now has.

And this is just the tip of the iceberg. There is so much more that God has done for us in and through Christ, things that call us to love him. He has given us his Holy Spirit to lead and guide us. He has given us his Word to instruct us. He has given us the fellowship of the saints to encourage us. He has given us the inestimable privilege of coming to his throne of grace in prayer.

Oh, how we should love Christ for all that he has done for us! Yes, every Christian loves Christ to some degree. Tell me you do not love Christ, and I will say without hesitation that you are not a Christian. But those of us who love Christ have ample and abundant reasons to love him to a greater degree than ever before.

What about those who are not children of God? What about those who do not yet love Christ? They also have abundant reasons for loving Christ. He came from heaven's glory to this earth to do what was necessary for our sins to be forgiven. He made it possible by his life and death for us to experience resurrection from the deadness of our sins. He is the one who will come again and take his people home to share his glory in heaven.

He now issues a warm and gracious invitation. He says 'whosoever will' may come and partake of this marvellous salvation he has provided.

In addition to all of that, this Lord who has provided everything necessary for you to be saved and this Lord who now graciously invites you to be saved also spares your life and gives you the opportunity to be saved. Yes, your times are in his hand. Every breath you take is a precious gift from his hand. It is by his good pleasure that you rise from your bed each morning and go about your work. Each day he allows you to do so gives you an additional opportunity to turn to him and to begin to love him.

Surely, we cannot read this account of Mary's love without thinking about this first question: do I love Christ as I ought?

What am I doing to show my love for Christ?

But Mary's act forces me to deal with another burning question, namely, what am I doing to show my love for Christ?

I do not doubt for a moment that there were others at that supper who loved Jesus. Jesus had twelve disciples and eleven of them had a true love for him. Martha certainly loved Christ and expressed it in helping to get the supper ready for him. But I think it is safe to say that no one else there loved Jesus like Mary did. The greatness of her love is proved by both the costliness of the gift and the openness with which she gave it.

Consider *the costliness of her gift*. The ointment, according to the assessment of Judas Iscariot, was worth three hundred denarii (v. 5). Commentators tell us that amount was nearly an entire year's wages for a working man! And she poured it all out on Jesus!

Then there was *her openness in giving it*. She could have done the same thing in the privacy of her own home with only her sister and brother present, but she did it in the presence of all Jesus' disciples and the other supper guests. She certainly knew she would be criticized for both the 'indecency' of loosing her hair and the costliness of the gift, but she was too absorbed with Jesus to care.

What are we doing to show our love for Christ? Are we giving sacrificially and openly as Mary did? Many think it is possible to love Christ without doing anything to show it. They limit love to feeling, but love always manifests itself in action.

How can we show our love for Christ? By worship. By giving sacrificially to his work. By openly expressing our faith in him even when it attracts scorn and ridicule from the Judases of this world. By ministering to those who are in need.

Mary has set a high standard. We can love Christ to a lesser degree, but we know in our heart of hearts that we ought to be striving to emulate Mary's example. If he has done no less for us than he did for her, we should settle for nothing less than her type of love.

Mary was not the only one that night to say something about this vital issue of loving Christ. Judas may not have realized it, but he answered these two questions that same night. His answer to the first was a resounding 'No!' and his answer to the second was a loud 'Nothing!' He professed to be shocked and indignant over such extravagant waste, and he wasted no time in letting everyone know that the ointment should have been sold and the proceeds given to the poor.

John lets us know Judas was not the champion of the poor he pretended to be (v. 6). His indignation was due to the fact that he saw a missed opportunity. If Mary had decided to give the ointment to the poor, she would almost certainly have asked Jesus to be the channel, and Jesus, in turn, would have asked Judas, the treasurer of the disciples, to sell the ointment. Judas could then have dipped into the proceeds and further feathered his own nest.

Judas had no love for Jesus at all and before the week was over sold him to the authorities for thirty pieces of silver. What a difference between Mary and Judas! She gave Jesus an offering that was worth two and a half times the amount Judas received for betraying him.

We have in Mary and Judas, then, differing answers on the question of loving Christ. May God help us to keep company with Mary and to love Christ with a fervent, unashamed love.

Notes

Introduction
1. D. Martyn Lloyd-Jones, *Saved in Eternity,* Crossway Books, pp.111-12.
2. John Bunyan, *The Pilgrim's Progress,* Zondervan Publishing House, p.40.
3. As above, p.41.
4. David Wells, *God in the Wasteland,* William B. Eerdmans Publishing Company, p.30.
5. David Kirkwood, *Christ's Incredible Cross,* Ethnos Press, p.106.

Chapter 2 — The cross needed: man's sin
1. John Murray, *Collected Writings of John Murray,* Banner of Truth, vol. ii, p.49.

Chapter 3 — The cross needed: God's holiness and wrath
1. John R. W. Stott, *Romans: God's Good News for the World,* InterVarsity Press, p.71.
2. John R. W. Stott, *The Cross of Christ,* InterVarsity Press, p.106.

Chapter 4 — A survey of Old Testament promises
1. *The Open Bible: The New King James Version,* Thomas Nelson Publishers, p.538.

Chapter 5 — A promise from the books of Moses
1. Michael Horton, *Putting Amazing Back into Grace,* Baker Book House, p.65.
2. Thomas Boston, *The Complete Works of Thomas Boston,* Richard Owen Roberts, Publishers, vol. vii, p.183.
3. Jonathan Edwards, *The Works of Jonathan Edwards,* The Banner of Truth Trust, vol. i, p.537.

Chapter 6 — A promise from the psalms
1. *New Geneva Study Bible: New King James Version,* Thomas Nelson Publishers, p.776.

Chapter 7 — A promise from the prophets
1. Stott, *The Cross*, p.145.
2. Roger Ellsworth, *A Promise is a Promise*, Evangelical Press, pp.34-5.

Chapter 8 — The cross typified: the institution of sacrifice
1. *Geneva Study Bible*, p.155.
2. Boston, *Works*, vol. vii, p.210.
3. Henry T. Mahan, *With New Testament Eyes: Genesis to Job*, Evangelical Press, p.11.
4. D. Martyn Lloyd-Jones, *Romans: Chapters 3:20 - 4:25*, Zondervan Publishing Company, p.88.

Chapter 10 — The work of Christ typified: a significant person
1. Edwards, *Works*, vol. i, p.554.
2. As above.

Chapter 11 — The Son arrives
1. Philip Hughes, *A Commentary on the Epistle to the Hebrews*, William B. Eerdmans Publishing Company, p.395.

Chapter 13 — The Son affirms the cross: in the wilderness
1. John MacArthur, *Matthew 1-7*, Moody Press, p.84.

Chapter 14 — The Son affirms the cross: in his public ministry
1. William Hendriksen, *New Testament Commentary: John*, Baker Book House, p.115.
2. Mahan, *With New Testament Eyes: Genesis to Job*, pp.70-71.

Chapter 15 — The Son affirms the cross: with his disciples
1. J. Glyn Owen, *From Simon to Peter*, Evangelical Press, p.130.

Chapter 16 — The Son affirms the cross: the transfiguration
1. R. C. Sproul, *Essential Truths of the Christian Faith*, Tyndale House Publishers, Inc., p.93.
2. Charles R. Eerdman, *The Gospel of Matthew*, The Westminster Press, p.136.
3. Sproul, *Essential Truths*, p.93.
4. Kent Hughes, *Mark*, Crossway Books, vol. ii, pp.15-16.
5. Owen, *From Simon to Peter*, p.147.
6. As above.

Chapter 18 — The Son affirms the cross: the upper room
1. John Brown, *Discourses and Sayings of our Lord Jesus Christ*, The Banner of Truth Trust, p.228.